NEWBURYPORT
AND THE
CIVIL WAR

★————————————————————★

NEWBURYPORT
AND THE
CIVIL WAR

★ ──────────────────────────── ★

WILLIAM HALLETT

Charleston · London

THE
History
PRESS

Published by The History Press
Charleston, SC 29403
www.historypress.net

Front: Frederick Douglass. *Library of Congress*; Caleb Cushing. *Author's collection*; Albert Pike. *Library of Congress*; USS *Marblehead*. *Naval Historical Center, Department of the Navy*. *Back*: Newburyport's Cushing Guard on State Street. *Historical Society of Old Newbury*. Atkinson Common postcard, early twentieth century. *Author's collection*.

First published 2012

Manufactured in the United States

ISBN 978.1.60949.448.3
Library of Congress Cataloging-in-Publication Data

Hallett, William.
Newburyport and the Civil War / William Hallett.
p. cm.
Includes bibliographical references and index.
ISBN 978-1-60949-448-3
1. Newburyport (Mass.)--History--19th century. 2. Massachusetts--History--Civil War, 1861-1865--Social aspects. 3. Newburyport (Mass.)--History, Military--19th century. 4. Newburyport (Mass.)--Social life and customs--19th century. 5. United States--History--Civil War, 1861-1865--Social aspects. I. Title.
F74.N55H18 2012
973.709744'5--dc23
2011046699

Contents

Preface   7

Chapter 1. William Lloyd Garrison   11
Chapter 2. Frederick Douglass's Visit   18
Chapter 3. Underground Operative   22
Chapter 4. A Notable Statesman   25
Chapter 5. Albert W. Bartlett and the Cushing Guards   30
Chapter 6. Ships and the Port   39
Chapter 7. Citizen Soldiers   46
Chapter 8. Not All Defended the Union   71
Chapter 9. Homefront Newburyport   79
Chapter 10. April 1865: Great News and Horrible News   87
Chapter 11. Yankee Homecoming   92
Chapter 12. Postwar Years   96

Conclusion   113
Notes   117
Bibliography   119
Index   125
About the Author   128

Preface

My earliest recollection of ever hearing the phrase "Civil War" was in my grandmother's kitchen on Bromfield Street. I must have been about five or so, and as I sat at the table, my father across from me and Gram by the sink, someone walked in (I believe my aunt) with a gift. It was a wooden music box with a diorama of a Confederate boy-soldier with a musket, a small cannon with cannonballs stacked and a small worm rail fence.

The adults began talking about the item, and though lacking details on the conversation, I do recall hearing words and phrases such as "blue," "gray," "brother against brother" and "Robert E. Lee." Even at this young age, I was curious about the brother-against-brother concept. I knew from family history what war was and that men who go to war might not come home.

Growing up with a strong interest in American history, it's not surprising that after visiting Gettysburg as an adult, I was bitten by the Civil War bug. This led me to reenacting, an involvement in Civil War roundtables, living histories, a collection of countless books (many I have yet to read!) and meeting with a variety of historians from all over.

People familiar with Newburyport, Massachusetts, know that just a ride or a walk immerses you in history. From High Street to Market Square, to the churches and the side streets with antique homes, the history is what draws people here from afar.

My wife, Elizabeth, and I were walking near downtown on some side streets one day, and I made a comment regarding the placards on some of the homes that described a certain captain or prominent citizen who lived there from dates about two hundred years ago or more. I remarked that these houses were here during the Civil War and that it's too bad that there isn't a listing or directory of the people from the Civil War—who they were and what they did.

Her reply was short, but it stopped me in my tracks and caused me to think. She asked, "Why don't you write it?" The result is the book you are currently holding. From the idea of a directory to a compilation of people and events, all connected with the Civil War and Newburyport, it became much more than I ever could have thought. The work on this book led me to meet new people, see artifacts and items that I didn't know existed and connect some of these people in Newburyport's history to my own family history.

I also learned that certain things that I thought were part of the history weren't. On the other side, many things that I didn't know were connected to Newburyport actually had ties, and sometimes in huge ways.

In compiling a book like this, certain parameters must be made. The book is called *Newburyport and the Civil War* after all. This excludes other neighboring towns, only because I wanted to keep the story focused. I omitted Fort Nichols at the mouth of the river because it's in Salisbury. I omitted heroes from Amesbury, Rowley, Ipswich and West Newbury (such as Ben Perley Poore). Caleb Huse could be argued as a Newbury resident, but though he was born in Newburyport and his father lived in Newburyport when the war broke out, it's only through his stepfamily that he's connected with the Coffin House—an abode just yards from the town line with Newburyport. In fact, one time Huse ran into Caleb Cushing on a train and mentioned how the two were from the same town. This book is only a sampling of people and events. The memorial at Atkinson Common lists more than 1,400 names, and I cover a fraction here.

Several people helped me in this effort. Cecile Pimental at the Newburyport Archival Center on Saturday mornings, along with Michael Bulger, offered some place to start and continued with tidbits of interest over time. Scott Nason not only became a new acquaintance but also allowed me to borrow an 1890 one-of-a-kind handwritten book from Newburyport's GAR Hall, which held a wealth of stories. Craig L. Symonds, professor emeritus of the U.S. Naval Academy, stopped me from going crazy trying to locate the *Merrimack* (there were more than twenty ships/boats named *Merrimack*) with one e-mail. Craig not only told me that the famous ship from the celebrated ironclad battle was actually built in Boston, not Newburyport, but also followed that by introducing me to Naval History and Command, the official history program from the Department of the Navy. These people are treasures, with information on many naval aspects and persons. Mark Bingham, a teacher and photographer in Portsmouth, was great at providing me with a photo I needed. Dick Simpson provided me with a great old book on Albert Pike. Another invaluable source of help was Paul Jancewicz. Jancy is a kindred spirit, and Liz and I know that any chat with him or visit will not be short, as we all love this history. Jancy had some wonderful information, and without him, this book would fall short. He is truly a great friend.

I must also thank Ghlee Woodworth for her help, ideas and advice on making books. The Historical Society of Old Newbury and the Massachusetts Historical Society both had wonderful photographs and samples, which are peppered throughout this book, but HSON had the local ones that made my jaw drop. Thanks, Jay Williamson! A late entry into the mix was a photo from Joe Callahan. It was a sharp, clear image, and I still find myself lost in the picture and the faces that look back.

One person above the others deserves the most thanks: my wife, Elizabeth. Her encouragement and support convinced me that I had the talent to write a book and fill a void in local history.

By the way, the song the wooden music box played, all those years ago, was "Dixie."

PHOTOGRAPHIC CREDITS

EH—photo by Elizabeth Hallett.
HSON—courtesy of the Historical Society of Old Newbury.
JC—courtesy of Joe Callahan.
LOC—courtesy of the Library of Congress.
MB—photo by Mark Bingham.
MHS—courtesy of the Massachusetts Historical Society.
NHC—courtesy of Naval Historical Center (Department of the Navy).
NPLAC—courtesy of Newburyport Public Library Archival Center.
WH—photo by William Hallett.
WHC—William Hallett Collection.

Chapter 1

William Lloyd Garrison

W illiam Lloyd Garrison didn't invent the abolitionist press or innovate the ideas, but he definitely accomplished the act of spreading the message on a national scale.

On December 10, 1805, William Lloyd Garrison was born on School Street in Newburyport, just behind the Old South Church. His parents, Abijah and Frances Maria (Lloyd), both from New Brunswick, Canada, would not see much of his life. In 1808, while William was a child, his father suddenly vanished from the picture, either dying at sea or leaving the family. His mother died on September 3, 1823, when he was not yet eighteen.

During his childhood, William's family was poor, reduced to knocking on backdoors of homes on High Street and other prominent residences and begging for leftovers. It may have been this experience that put him in a sympathetic mind for those less fortunate.

Before his mother's death, he tried various trades to make a living. Before his tenth birthday, he was apprenticed in Lynn to a shoemaker. In less than a year, he and his mother moved to Baltimore, Maryland. This, too, did not last long, as a year later, in 1816, he was back in Newburyport. He was apprenticed to a cabinetmaker in Haverhill in 1818 but returned the same year to Newburyport and was apprenticed to Ephraim W. Allen, editor of the *Newburyport Herald*.

While working at the *Herald*, Garrison began to show his skill. Caleb Cushing, who was a contributing writer for the *Newburyport Herald*, saw some of Garrison's writing and encouraged him to write more, thinking highly of

From humble beginnings in this house on School Street where he was born, William Lloyd Garrison would not rest in his fight against causes such as slavery. *WHC.*

his skill. He began to write anonymously and for other papers as well. His time with Mr. Allen ended in 1825, and William was ready to begin his new job in 1826 as editor of the *Free Press* of Newburyport. It was about this time that he met John Greenleaf Whittier—a friendship that would last him his life.

In January 1828, Garrison began working in Boston as a journeyman printer and worked as editor of the *National Philanthropist*. Later the same year, he started a paper in Bennington, Vermont, called the *Journal of the Times*, which endorsed John Quincy Adams for president. He was very outspoken about reform in the form of both abolitionism and temperance.

Garrison next took his case to Baltimore, with friend Benjamin Lundy, to establish an antislavery paper in the lion's den—not only was Maryland a slave state, but Baltimore was also one of the larger slave markets in the slave trade. The people of Baltimore were not too fond of the "Madcap" Garrison.

One day, a ship from Newburyport, Massachusetts, arrived in Baltimore for the purpose of transporting slaves to New Orleans. This made Garrison furious, and he denounced the event. Mr. Francis Todd, the owner, sued Garrison for libel. Mr. Todd of Newburyport claimed to not have known that slaves would be the cargo, but the captain claimed otherwise. Garrison said that the only error in his story was that the ship held eighty-five slaves and not seventy-five. He was found guilty by a jury of slave owners and fined fifty dollars. As he could not afford the fine, he was sent to jail. This move was met with exclamations of joy in the South, while in the North many were feeling just the opposite. Garrison was in jail for forty-nine days until his fine was paid for by Arthur Toppan of New York.

Garrison and Lundy began to argue over the direction of the paper and the idea of colonization. Garrison packed his things and headed back to Boston to begin his antislavery newspaper, the *Liberator*, with the first issue being published in January 1831. He was very harsh in his words about slavery, the slave trade and the government's lack of action. At about this time, he also severed all connection with Newburyport, likely due to Newburyport's business with slave states and the population's support of business over principles.

The *Liberator* debuted in early 1831. A year later, the New England Anti-Slavery Society was formed, one of the cofounders being William Lloyd Garrison. Joshua Coffin of Newbury and Isaac Knapp and Michael Simpson of Newburyport were among the twelve members who established the organization.

Garrison was an active abolitionist to say the least. Over the years before the Civil War, he pushed for Massachusetts to secede from the Union and break ties with slaveholders, he was a delegate to the anti-Texas convention at Faneuil Hall and he spoke at many antislavery meetings throughout New England and the rest of the country. He met John Brown when Brown was wanted for the murders of proslavery men in Kansas but before Brown's raid at Harpers Ferry. He met and was briefly friends with Frederick Douglass. Frederick Douglass even said that it was after watching Garrison give one of his antislavery speeches that Douglass knew that he, too, wanted to be an orator.

Life for Garrison in Newburyport was not as welcoming as one might think. As Newburyport was a busy commercial port trying to regain its financial footing after President Jefferson's embargo, and also recovering from the Great Fire of 1811, people needed all the trade they could get, and a large amount came from southern states. Business trumped social causes.

During one visit to the meetinghouse on Titcomb Street on Brown Square (North Church), Garrison gave a speech that made many in the audience disruptive and caused the hosts to refuse any further visits from Mr. Garrison. There may have been other influences at work, as Francis Todd had previously intervened when Garrison attempted to speak at the Harris Street meetinghouse. Mr. Todd was still not fond of Garrison and held the grudge from Baltimore.

North Church on Brown Square was not pleased with William Lloyd Garrison and told him not to return. Years later, a statue of Garrison was placed within yards of the front door. *WHC.*

Boston was not completely behind the abolitionists either—one time, when Garrison went to speak at the Female Anti-Slavery Society meeting, a mob grabbed him. His clothes were ripped and his hat taken. A noose awaited Garrison, and he was only saved at the last minute. Although never proven, it was often circulated among groups that Boston mayor Theodore Lyman may have been behind the frightful night. He was a member of a proslavery group meeting at Faneuil Hall and had guests from the South that night.

During this period in Boston history, Irish immigrants were coming in waves and settling into their new lives. Irish were typically considered the lowest in society and, fearful of jobs that any freed men of color might take, were very much against the abolitionist groups. Garrison found it difficult to find any venues at which he could speak or hold rallies.

On January 31, 1865, with slavery all but history, the members of the New England Anti-Slavery Society deemed no reason to continue and disbanded. At the end of March that year, William Lloyd Garrison was in Newburyport addressing a crowd at city hall. He referred to his time there and to the antislavery movement. He couldn't help but mention his conflict with Francis Todd. He reminded the citizenry how he had been refused the chance to lecture; just five years before, he would have been "kicked out of the city." He gave thanks to his friend John Greenleaf Whittier and read a hymn by the poet. He stated that he had come this time at the request of the people of Newburyport, and he made a prophetic statement when he claimed that one day Newburyport would be proud of him.

The day that the Stars and Stripes was hoisted over Fort Sumter, just days after Lee's surrender to Grant, Garrison was on hand to witness the flag ripple in the Charleston Harbor breeze. He was there with Governor Andrew and other dignitaries.

The year 1865 saw the last issue of the *Liberator*, published in December, just months after William Lloyd Garrison resigned from the American Anti-Slavery Society. He turned his attention to other causes, such as the prohibition of alcohol, which was now gaining in popularity. But he never quit writing against the things he felt strongly about when it came to how the South was now being treated. He protested Robert E. Lee's position at Washington College, and when President Hayes formally announced that he would withdraw troops from the Southern states, ending the occupation and consequentially ending Reconstruction as well, Garrison attacked that decision with the same intensity he had in his younger days.

Garrison died in New York on May 24, 1879. His remains were returned to Massachusetts, where he was interred at Forest Hills Cemetery in Roxbury.

History has a sense of humor, as Garrison, not liked by the majority of Newburyporters, would get a statue in his honor by that very city. William Harris Swasey was a man of great generosity. He wanted to honor a Newburyporter, and Garrison was just the man. Swasey funded the statue. At first, Mr. Swasey thought of donating a fountain to honor Mr. Garrison, but then he thought that a statue in Brown Square, near the church that hadn't wanted Garrison to speak, would be a great place for it. In March 1893, Swasey wrote:

> *To the Honorable, the Mayor, and the City Council of the City of Newburyport*
>
> *Gentlemen—our townsman Mr. D.M. French has in his studio a colossal statue of the late William Lloyd Garrison, which I would be pleased to put in bronze and present to the city of Newburyport to be erected in one of its public parks*
>
> *Your Obedient Servant,*
> *William H. Swasey*[1]

By the twentieth century, the statue of William Lloyd Garrison in Brown Square was revered by most of the population, who considered him heroic—quite contrary to how citizens of Newburyport had depicted him throughout most of his life. *WHC.*

David M. French lived on Washington Street between Strong and Olive Streets with his wife, Harriet. Born in Newmarket, New Hampshire, he moved to Newburyport in 1864 after achieving a fine reputation in Portsmouth for his busts and other carvings. After moving to Newburyport, he easily found work. He executed works of many Newburyporters, such as Josiah Little, founder of the Public Library; Caleb Cushing; John Greenleaf Whittier of Amesbury; William H. Huse; and members of the Moseley family. He felt, though, that the Garrison statue was his crowning accomplishment.

Working from his studio at 44 Pleasant Street in the Philips Building (located across from the current post office), French created the statue from more than 1,200 pounds of clay, working from only one photograph. The rest was from the best research he could do. Swasey commissioned French in November 1892.

Unfortunately, when the *New York Times* covered this story, it mistook David M. French for another New Hampshire artist, Daniel Chester French. The two are not related. But nonetheless, the day of the unveiling was for William Lloyd Garrison. On July 4, 1893, an Independence Day not to be forgotten, a large procession wound its way through the streets. A parade and thousands of people joined the mayor, members of the city council and others in honoring Garrison.

Garrison once wrote a sonnet to Newburyport:

"To My Birthplace"

Whether a persecuted child of thine
Thou deign to own, my lovely place
In characters that time cannot efface,
Thy worth is graved upon this heart of mine.
Forsake me not in anger, nor repine
That with this nation I am in disgrace;
From ruthless bondage to redeem my race,
And save my country is my great design.
How much soe'er my conduct thou dost blame,
For hate and calumny belie my course,
My labors shall not sully thy fair fame;
But thy shall be to thee a fountain source
Of joyfulness hereafter—when my name
Shall e-en from tyrants a just tribute force.[2]

The statue was dedicated near the meetinghouse where the ruckus had been years before and in front of the city hall. The *New York Times* described the statue's pose as if Garrison were addressing an audience: "If it is a typical audience he is addressing, there are interruptions and threats of bodily injury, to all of which Garrison was wont to present a calm front, convinced as he was that his views were not only right and on the right side of mercy, but essential in their working-out to the safety and well-being of the land."[3]

Chapter 2

Frederick Douglass's Visit

It's widely known that Massachusetts had the reputation as being full of abolitionists in the antebellum years of American history. Much of that is based on the likes of people such as William Lloyd Garrison, but also on the many conductors with the Underground Railroad.

Many people in the twenty-first century might believe that with such an antislavery reputation, people welcomed men of color. This was not the case, and the state resembled much the way the South would behave after the war and for half of the twentieth century.

Two men came traveling through New England on what we would call a lecture circuit. The men, Frederick Douglass and John A. Collins of Boston, were out to rally antislavery emotions and add to their numbers. Collins encouraged Douglass to tell his story and to tell the facts. This mode of lecturing would be echoed by Douglass's then friend, William Lloyd Garrison.

Douglass was an escaped slave from Baltimore, and many people, especially those not familiar with seeing slavery or African Americans, were amazed at his expressiveness and how he spoke as an educated man would.

In August 1841, Douglass began his career as a speaker. In Abington on September 4, members of the antislavery society there said that his style was "eloquent and affecting."[4] They added that his "masterly manner" in the subject was "full of interest."

In a few days, the gentlemen were in Newburyport. On Tuesday, September 7, 1841, at 7:30 p.m. at the Temple Street Church (situated

Frederick Douglass, former slave turned public speaker, came to Newburyport in 1841 and spoke against slavery in one of his first tours of New England. *LOC.*

between Prospect Street, Fair Street and Temple Street), a crowd gathered to hear the men talk. Frederick Douglass, who had learned to read from the wife of his owner, was becoming a powerful speaker for the cause of abolitionism and earned a reputation that spread throughout the nation. The topic this night was titled "American Slavery."

Left: John A. Collins, an abolitionist from Boston, accompanied Frederick Douglass to Newburyport in 1841 when Douglass was making his first tour of New England. While sitting next to Mr. Collins, Douglass was told by the conductor to move to the back of the train. *MHS.*

Below: The Temple Street meetinghouse was located on Prospect and Fair Streets, with the back side along Temple Street. Here, accompanied by John A. Collins, Frederick Douglass spoke on the evils of slavery. The building burned down in the early twentieth century. *NPLAC.*

It was likely that on this visit Mr. Douglass was entertained at the home of Richard Plumer, who lived on Federal Street. It was highly probable that local inns wouldn't have accepted Douglass at their establishments.

The next day, Wednesday, September 8, the two men continued their journey with a planned engagement in Dover, New Hampshire. There was to be the annual meeting of the Strafford County Anti-Slavery Society. While on the train from Newburyport to Portsmouth, Douglass refused to give up his seat next to his friend Collins. The Eastern Railroad's policy created a separate car for freed men of color. Douglass was roughed up a bit, but only some tears in his clothing and a few bruises were the outcome by the time he was in Dover.

Chapter 3

Underground Operative

If you went to the post office in 1871, it was located at 38 State Street, at the corner of State and Threadneedle Alley. Most people would know it these days by the old Coca-Cola ad faintly visible from a time gone by.

The postmaster was a man named Richard Plumer. Plumer was known to many in town as the man who owned and ran a dry goods store at 46 State Street, not far from the post office, just a few doors down. Plumer was a fairly well-known man, as his business was on Newburyport's busy thoroughfare, but only a few years earlier, he had been involved in undertakings that few in town or the surrounding area knew about.

Although most of Newburyport residents were against getting involved in the slavery issue, since so much commerce revolved around the port, some, like Richard Plumer, were involved in the Underground Railroad.

This type of operation was not of the iron, coal and steam railroad, but rather it was a secretive system of aiding escaped slaves coming from the South heading to free soil. For years, getting slaves north of the Mason-Dixon line was all it took, until the Fugitive Slave Act was enacted in 1851. The southern states, which extolled the importance of states' rights, had no problem with this federal law, which allowed slave catchers and other authorities to capture escaped slaves in any state, even the free states of the North, and return them to slavery. The slaves' only recourse was to head to Canada, which meant a longer road to safety and freedom.

Richard Plumer used his house at number 69 (now 73) Federal Street, as well as other means, to help slaves escape. People could not know what he

Right: The unassuming businessman with a dry goods store on State Street, Richard Plumer of Newburyport was actually an agent for the Underground Railroad. *MHS*.

Below: Richard Plumer used his home on Federal Street to do his part in the Underground Railroad and also to supply Frederick Douglass with accommodations on his visit to Newburyport. *EH*.

was doing or he would likely face criminal charges. To transport the slaves, Plumer or a family member would guide their wagon down High Road in Newbury to the bridge at the Parker River. The slaves would be covered and hidden as best as possible. From there, they could be taken to Plumer's home for a time or directly to the next operative, who could have been William Jackman on the northern edge of Newbury in what is now Newburyport. It also could be at the Chain Bridge where friends of John Greenleaf Whittier of Amesbury would have continued the job. On occasion, Plumer took the slaves to the Turkey Hill section of Newburyport to meet with Robert Brown and people of West Newbury who would help. This kind of work required that a man keep from having a constant routine. Plumer also took escaping slaves to the Coffin House near the border with Newbury.

Perhaps word among the Underground Railroad operators and abolitionists led to Plumer having Frederick Douglass as a house guest. As was mentioned, Mr. Douglass visited Newburyport in September 1841, and with the prejudiced feelings of most people at the time, it was likely that Mr. Douglass would have needed a place to stay, as locations such as the Wolfe Tavern or other inns in Newburyport would not have welcomed his race.

If you travel down Federal Street today, the red house at no. 73 is proudly adorned with a plaque noting the historic connection between Richard Plumer and Frederick Douglass.

Chapter 4

A Notable Statesman

I n 1860, the political arena was thick with action. The whole country was simmering with an assortment of men looking to sway others to their party or point of view. Opposing groups were already talking about what to do should this or that party take control.

Caleb Cushing was born in Salisbury, Massachusetts, in 1800; he was only two when his family moved to Newburyport, which he would call home until his death. The Cushing family made their fortune on shipping. John, Caleb's father, owned numerous ships, and goods came and went all over the world. Caleb went to Harvard and, not long afterward, began practicing law. Shipping was still a large form of income for the family, and many of the ports they used were in southern locales.

Mr. Cushing became an outstanding member of Newburyport and, upon the deaths of John Adams and Thomas Jefferson on July 4, 1826, was asked to give eulogies in public for the people who grieved for these two founders. In 1835, General Lafayette died, and Cushing was asked to speak of the famous aide to Washington in Dover, New Hampshire. His speech was later printed and distributed throughout the region.

Being for states' rights and with friends and interests in the South, it's no surprise that Cushing was opposed to the abolitionist movement that was growing in his home state of Massachusetts. However, his ties to both places gave him opportunities that many others didn't have.

Cushing went to war during the conflict with Mexico as a general and came home with enough clout that soon the local Newburyport Militia had changed its name to the Cushing Guards. In the years before the Civil War, he was a member of the Massachusetts House of Representatives, an ambassador to China (replacing former governor and orator Edward Everett), mayor of Newburyport and attorney general under President Franklin Pierce.

It was while serving in Washington circles, and highly likely while in Pierce's cabinet, that he became very close friends with a southern gentleman named Jefferson Davis. Davis, from Mississippi, was secretary of war under Pierce, had also served in the Mexican-American War and was an accomplished statesman in his own right.

Jefferson Davis traveled and visited Caleb Cushing at his home at 63 High Street. The men were like brothers, and during one visit in October 1858, when Mr. Davis was to speak at Faneuil Hall in Boston, it was Caleb Cushing who introduced him to the audience.

Seen here in his prime, Caleb Cushing was one of Newburyport's highly esteemed businessmen, politicians and heroes. Politics of the day may have been the reason Cushing was refused his offer to Governor Andrew at the outset of the war. *MHS.*

All events seemed to come to a head with the election year of 1860. The Democrats, to which Cushing aligned himself, had their convention in Charleston, South Carolina, on April 23. Caleb Cushing was the chairman of the convention. But even among these members of the same party, no one could agree to anything, and the convention was disbanded on May 3 with no one chosen.

A second attempt took place in Baltimore, and Cushing was at the top of the list for nominees. Why not? He was a northerner with ties to the South. His ships often carried cotton, and as a lawyer, he was well acquainted with many in law and politics. Still, the debate was heated, and Cushing withdrew himself from nomination, leaving the door open for Stephen A. Douglas to be the Democrat to beat in November.

That November, however, Abraham Lincoln won the election, setting off a chain of events before he took office on March 4, 1861, in which many

Left: Jefferson Davis, secretary of war under President Pierce, was so close to Caleb Cushing that he wrote regarding the parting of his friend in 1861: "[W]hen we parted it was like taking the last leave of a brother." Photo by Mathew Brady. *LOC*.

Below: Cushing's home on High Street once welcomed Jefferson Davis, senator from Mississippi, who would later become the president of the Confederate States of America. *WH*.

27

Southern states left the Union, forming the Confederate States of America. All Lincoln could do was wait.

In January 1861, Jefferson Davis wrote a letter to former president Pierce, explaining Mississippi's vote on secession and how hard it was for him to leave his association with friends in the Union: "When Lincoln comes in he will have but to continue in the path of his predecessor to inaugurate a civil war and, leave a so distant democratic administration responsible for the fact. Genl Cushing was here last week and when we parted it seemed like taking a last leave of a Brother."[5]

On February 18, 1861, two weeks before Lincoln took his oath of office, Jefferson Davis was sworn in as the president of the Confederate States of America.

Cushing offered his services to Governor John A. Andrew, as his experience in the Mexican-American War surely would have been to the Union's advantage. Andrew declined his offer, likely due to a feeling of questionable loyalty—also, Andrew was an abolitionist and Cushing was not. However, the question of politics comes in as well, as Cushing had endorsed Benjamin F. Butler for governor in the 1860 election that Andrew had won. Andrew's

After serving his country and his home of Newburyport for most of his life, Cushing died just shy of his seventy-ninth birthday and was laid to rest at New Hill Cemetery. *WH.*

reply to Cushing was curt: "Were I to accept your offer, I would dishearten numerous good and loyal men and tend to demoralize our military service."[6]

In fact, as the war began, Lincoln was set to commission Caleb Cushing, but Governor Andrew talked Lincoln out of it. Butler, who became a general in the Civil War and achieved his own fame, had recommended Cushing's appointment and felt that it was a serious mistake not using Cushing's experience.

Still, in 1864, Lincoln called on Mr. Cushing to help in a commission to go to Great Britain and resolve some claims presented by the European island. Cushing continued to serve in many diplomatic roles for Presidents Johnson and Grant and was part of the Treaty of Washington of 1871, which improved relations between the United States and Canada.

Cushing's name was brought up for the Supreme Court, but many Republicans still couldn't forgive him for his anti-abolitionist views. He was denied this post. In the late 1870s, he returned home to Newburyport, keeping busy with legal matters up until his death on January 2, 1879.

Chapter 5

Albert W. Bartlett
and the Cushing Guards

The Bartlett surname has a long history in Newburyport. John Bartlett, Christopher Bartlett and Richard Bartlett are listed as among the original proprietors of the town of Newbury in 1642. The name is woven throughout the history of Newburyport.

In 1861, one of the Bartletts found himself ready to answer Mr. Lincoln's call for volunteers. Albert Wood Bartlett was boarding at a house on Winter Street (the building no longer stands) and was making a name in local politics. He was born on August 18, 1832. He lived with his wife, Harriet B. Bartlett, and had a young daughter, Harriet, who was seven years old at the time. His younger brother, Edward, lived at 147 Water Street and worked for Albert in dry goods.

Mayor Moses Davenport died on February 18, 1861, and George W. Jackman Jr. was elected by the city council on February 27. It was under this administration that Albert W. Bartlett worked as a representative for Ward 4.

Ward 4 jurisdiction ran from the middle of State Street to the middle of Winter Street, and it continued to the southwestern end of the city. Three men spoke for the people of Ward 4: Charles M. Hodge, Albert W. Bartlett and Charles H. Titcomb.

Along with his civic politics, Albert was a member of the Cushing Guards. To understand this group, one must understand local militias. Every town or city in the nineteenth century had local militias. The men would attend appointed meetings and perhaps do some drilling, but mostly they were

The men of the Cushing Guards of Newburyport donned their old uniforms and marched up State Street before the Civil War. *HSON.*

treated as social clubs. When times became serious, though, local militias throughout the United States would be called into service.

On March 2, 1861, two days before Abraham Lincoln took the oath of office, Captain Nehemiah Flanders resigned as head of the Cushing Guards. As his popularity in Newburyport had grown, Albert W. Bartlett was elected first lieutenant, which was how leaders in militias were usually chosen.

It wasn't long after President Lincoln took office that the crisis at Fort Sumter in Charleston Harbor began. With tensions building between the Southern forces and what they deemed an unwelcome presence, the first shots were fired at about 4:30 a.m. on April 12, 1861. Abraham Lincoln called for seventy-five thousand volunteers from the loyal states to put down the rebellion on April 15, the same day Fort Sumter surrendered.

The *Newburyport Daily Herald* on April 16, 1861, printed this message from Benjamin Butler of Lowell:

> *General B.F. Butler of Lowell means to retrieve the honor he lost at the Charleston Convention. He avows his intention of supporting the Administration in the war for the preservation of the Union, and asks to be*

called into service. He says that he who hangs back now is a traitor to his country, and should be dealt with accordingly.[7]

One of the first units of Massachusetts to answer the president's call was the Cushing Guards of Newburyport, under the leadership of Albert W. Bartlett. These men became part of the Eighth Massachusetts Regiment, Company A, and were called to serve three-month enlistments. Everyone thought, or at least hoped, that this would be plenty of time to end this trouble in the South.

Capt. Albert W. Bartlett
Commander Company A

The 8th Regiment is ordered to march to the defense of the capital. Will rendezvous in Faneuil Hall to-morrow. How many men will you muster?

(signed) Edward W. Hinks, adjutant[8]

Bartlett had to ready his men. He told them, "Men, my orders are to appear in Boston, whether with few men or many. I must go. Be ready to march."[9] The men who left with Bartlett were Lieutenant George Barker, Lieutenant G. Hodges, Lieutenant George Creasey and Sergeants Thomas E. Marshall and Nathan W. Collins. There were also the following privates: Horace W. Bartlett, Joseph Barlow, Samuel Baxter, William H. Dodge, Richard S. Dodge, John S. Frost, Nathan R. Giles, Sanford W. Grant, Stephen H. Goodwin, Joseph L. Johnson, Thomas E. Lang, Charles P. Morrison, John A. Perley, Joseph L. Shaw and Richard van Moll.

It was a cold day with rain and sleet on April 16 when the Eighth Massachusetts set out for Boston. Not everyone was ready for the eight o'clock train, but they were for the twelve o'clock one. The crowd that gathered was rather quiet, and there were few cheers and fewer words as family and friends waved goodbye to the men of the new regiment.

The other companies that filled out the rest of the regiment's number consisted of Company B (Lafayette Guard) and Company C (Sutton Light Infantry), both of Marblehead, along with Company H (Glover Light Guards). Lynn supplied Company D (Light Infantry) and Company F (City Guards). Company E (Light Infantry) was from Beverly. Company G (American Guard) was from Gloucester. Salem offered a Zouave group known as a well-trained group, Company I (Light Infantry). Finally,

One of the original Cushing Guards who left to go defend the Union, George Barker. New Hill Cemetery. *WH.*

Company K (Allen Guard) was the only western band, as they came from Pittsfield.

On April 18, the regiment was presented the colors at a ceremony in front of the statehouse, with Governor Andrew sending it off with words of encouragement, citing Massachusetts as once more being the "inspiration of historic American liberty."

After the governor's speech, General Benjamin Butler stood before the soldiers and the crowd and continued with the upbeat, patriotic fervor: "Sons of Puritans, who believe in the providence of Almighty God! As He was with our fathers, so may He be with us in this strife for the right."[10]

It was four o'clock in the afternoon when the Eighth left Boston for Worcester and Springfield, where the men picked up their Pittsfield comrades, and it was the morning of April 19 when they arrived in New York City to cheers as they marched down Broadway.

Later that afternoon, they arrived in Philadelphia and heard the news of the Sixth Massachusetts's attempts at passing through Baltimore and the mob that attacked them in what is now known as the Pratt Street Riot.

Baltimore was a hotbed of Confederate thought and became a hostile city on April 19 as the Sixth Regiment, made up from men from Lawrence and Lowell, attempted to cross from President Street depot to Camden Station on its way to Washington. A mob taunted the men, and eventually gunshots rang out, with casualties on both sides. It was the first bloodshed of the war.

So the decision was made to bypass Baltimore. As the Eighth entered Maryland, the men took a steamer called *Maryland* down to Annapolis from Havre de Grace. When the regiment arrived in Annapolis, one of the first duties was to secure the USS *Constitution*. The ship had been a training vessel used by midshipmen of the U.S. Naval Academy, and Butler feared losing the ship (for practical as well as symbolic reasons). Taking it in tow, Company H sailed "Old Ironsides" to New York. While in Annapolis, it is likely that the regiment's presence helped to sway the Maryland legislature to vote to remain in the Union.

By the end of April, the remainder of the Cushing Guards who weren't able to come on such short notice caught up with the Eighth Regiment, Company A. It wasn't long afterward that Albert received a promotion. On April 30, he was mustered in as captain of Company A.

The next task for the Eighth was to repair the railroad between Annapolis and Washington. Once in the capital, they were reviewed by President Lincoln and then quartered in the Rotunda of the unfinished domed Capitol building, where they traded their fancy uniforms for the standard blue that Uncle Sam gave to all his soldiers.

The Eighth was also sent just west of Baltimore on May 28, to the town of Relay, Maryland, to provide security for the Baltimore and Ohio Railroad. General Butler was put in command of this region and needed to keep Baltimore safe for Federal troops and secure railroads. Only one rail line fed Washington from the North, and it came from Baltimore on the B&O Railroad. The men then went to Baltimore on June 17 and stayed there for about six weeks.

By Thursday, August 1, 1861, the men had served their three months and were welcomed back as heroes. They were paraded through the main downtown streets to cheers from people of Newburyport, and eventually the parade ended with a banquet, hosted by Captain John Moore of the Veterans Artillery Association. The men were then mustered out.

Both Lieutenant George Barker and Captain Albert W. Bartlett opened recruiting offices in Market Square. Barker was refilling the ranks for Hinks. But Albert was looking to form up another regiment with Newburyport men—and he did. Company B of the Thirty-fifth Massachusetts Infantry

The Eighth Massachusetts Regiment was put to work in repairing crucial railroad lines, as depicted in this rendering from *Frank Lesley's Illustrated Newspaper*. *LOC.*

THE EIGHTH MASSACHUSETTS REGIMENT IN THE ROTUNDA OF THE CAPITOL, WASHINGTON.—[See Page 331.]

When the Eighth Massachusetts arrived in Washington, the men were quartered in the Rotunda of the Capitol. This image was published in *Harper's Weekly*. *LOC.*

A true "Yankee Homecoming" took place on August 1, 1861, as the Eighth Massachusetts, Company A, marched down State Street past the Woart-Moseley-Stone House (now Woart-Perkins House), with throngs of cheering Newburyporters along the way. *JC.*

was formed up, and Albert W. Bartlett was mustered as captain on August 8, 1862, just ten days before his thirtieth birthday.

This regiment arrived in time to serve in the IX Corps of the Army of the Potomac, with General Ambrose Burnside commanding. It was only a few weeks later that the men would fight in the Battle of South Mountain on September 14, 1862, in western Maryland, which was only a prelude to the Battle of Antietam just three days later.

The overall commander of the Army of the Potomac was General George B. McClellan. A friend of Burnside's, McClellan at one point ordered Burnside to take his men across Antietam Creek to a bluff, where a small group of 350 Georgian Confederates were holed up. Many places along the creek allowed for various crossing possibilities, but Burnside decided that the Rohrbach Bridge was important to take. After some time, the Thirty-fifth, the regiment with little experience, was thrust into the battle after men from

Right: Captain Albert W. Bartlett (the only known photo) led the first heroes from Newburyport. Later, while in the Thirty-fifth Massachusetts, Company B, he was killed in action at Burnside's Bridge at the Battle of Antietam. *WHC.*

Below: Not long after the Battle of Antietam, Alexander Gardner photographed the now infamous Burnside's Bridge over Antietam Creek. *LOC.*

Pennsylvania, New Hampshire and others. It was at this time, in this area, that Captain Albert W. Bartlett of Newburyport was killed in action by what apparently were four severe wounds received simultaneously. Along with Bartlett, other Newburyporters from Company B who died near Burnside's Bridge, as it would forever be known, were David R. Hinkley, Alphonso P. Reed, Caleb C. Pike, George W. Hodgdon, William C. Colby, Joseph Cossar, Jeremiah Long Jr. and musician Benjamin Hazen Rogers, born in Byfield.

The Thirty-fifth Massachusetts, Company B, went into battle to take the bridge with a line of 775 men. When the day was done, 214 were lost.

Captain Bartlett's body was returned to Newburyport. Services were held at the Pleasant Street Church, and this young man with such civic pride and service was buried at Oak Hill Cemetery with full military honors.

Albert's younger brother, Edward, also served in the war. He was in the Cushing Guards later on and, after a time, also served in the Sixtieth Massachusetts at Forts Lee and Pickering in Salem Harbor. His grave in Oak Hill is nothing more than a small cube with the initials "E.F.B."

Chapter 6

Ships and the Port

Any discussion or thought of Newburyport and the Civil War cannot be considered complete without the reason why the city exists: the port.

When the people along the Merrimack River realized that the rural hills and fields of Newbury did not meet their needs, they broke from old Newbury and formed Newbury Port in 1764. By 1851, the charter had become a city.

The life of Newburyport absolutely revolved around the Merrimack River as it meets the Atlantic at Newburyport. Industry, trade and fishing, as well as all of the businesses owing to those trades for their livelihoods, were all located along the waterfront. The view we have now certainly does not resemble the waterfront of the nineteenth century. Where there were shipyards, there were also sail makers, coopers, rope makers and all of the other needs that ships require for voyages on the open ocean. Then there were warehouses for receiving goods from far away or for awaiting ships to take them to far-off ports.

George W. Jackman Jr. owned one of the most successful shipyards along the river, located along Merrimac Street near the end of Forrester Street. Jackman himself lived on Woodland Street near High Street. Jackman's success and involvement in town took him to the position of head of city hall when Mayor Moses Davenport died on February 18, 1861. The city council chose Jackman as the next mayor, putting him in the post just as the war was to begin. He was also mayor at the end of the war. With a short break in the middle of the war, when Isaac Boardman held the position, Jackman was the Civil War mayor.

The Newburyport waterfront of the nineteenth century was not the tourist-aimed place of today. Shipyards and the businesses that relied on them dotted the shore of the Merrimack River from downtown to the Chain Bridge. *WHC.*

Jackman continued to manage his shipbuilding business even as mayor of Newburyport. He had, before the war, been postmaster of the Newburyport Post Office, which was located at 38 State Street at the corner with Threadneedle Alley.

Newburyport, as with most of the Northern cities and states, relied on shipping for its survival. The Southern states were quite aware of this fact, and early on in the war, the Confederacy enacted a plan to wreak havoc on the North by attacking merchant vessels, certainly harming the Northern economy.

One of the most famous of these ships was the CSS *Alabama*. Built in Liverpool, England, by John Laird Sons and Company, it was commissioned on August 24, 1862, and helmed by Captain Raphael Semmes. Many of Newburyport's ships were targeted by Captain Semmes. On March 25, 1863, the 699-ton *Charles Hill*, built in Newburyport, was burned and sunk off the coast of Brazil. The *Jabez Snow*, a 1,074-ton ship, was captured and burned with its load of coal on May 29, 1863.

The *Sonora* left Newburyport and spent some time in New York Harbor, and then in March 1863, it traveled to Melbourne, following that with a trip to Hong Kong. The *Sonora*'s captain, Lawrence W. Brown, noted what an odd sight it was that at least twenty-five American ships were in the harbor yet had what appeared to be little plan of moving. He soon found out that the raider the *Alabama* was in the China Seas waiting for American ships. The ships had been staying put for weeks.

The journey continued as they went to Akyab, India, for rice destined for Europe. After a brief stop in Singapore, the *Sonora* continued. On a fateful day, December 26, 1863, Captain Brown noticed a steamer heading in their direction flying a blue British ensign. The steamer came alongside, and in a very gentlemanly way, the crew of the *Sonora* was ordered to transfer the goods to the steamer, which had identified itself as the Confederate ship *Alabama*.

Captain Brown was taken to the *Alabama*, and in his words, the crew lacked discipline, and he was not impressed with the operation, as it seemed much disorganized. Finally, he was sent to Captain Semmes's quarters. Semmes requested information about the cargo, the destination and where the ship was registered. Captain Brown was not impressed with Semmes and didn't think highly of him. For now, the *Sonora* was in tow.

An intense dialogue took place between the two captains. Semmes gave Brown the option of staying on the *Alabama* for eight to ten days until they reached a port, at which point he'd be dropped off. Option number two was for Brown to be set adrift with his crew of mixed races. Captain Brown told Semmes that his men, both white and black, and his officers had been loyal and true and that his duty was with them. He would go through whatever they would: "I know my duty."[11]

Upon arriving back on deck, Captain Brown observed the *Alabama* crew acting boastful, as though they had caught a fleet of warships and not a single innocent merchant ship. "It seemed to me like an eagle swooping down on a humming bird," he said.[12]

Brown and his crew, including First Officer Isaac Colby and Second Officer Bradford Swap, both of Newburyport, were let loose and watched the *Sonora* burn until it sank. They managed to get to the island of Penang on December 31, and since Captain Semmes hadn't checked Captain Brown's person, Brown divvied up the money that he had stashed, giving each man $100 with which to make his way home. Each man was on his own now. Captain Brown took a number of ships until a German ship took him to New York. Lawrence Brown finally arrived back in Newburyport on March 17, 1864.

The *Alabama* inflicted considerable damage on Northern shipping, as was its goal. It is said that it captured more than sixty ships and prizes totaling about $6 million—all in about two years of service.

Up the road from Newburyport is the Portsmouth Naval Shipyard. It was there where a ship (later named the USS *Kearsarge*) was built that would pursue the *Alabama*. Finally battling off the coast of Cherbourg, France, on June 19, 1864, after about an hour, the *Kearsarge* was the sure victor, as the Confederacy's prized raider sank. Among the crew of the *Kearsarge* was George W. Remick, born in Newburyport on February 28, 1821. George had enlisted in Portsmouth in January 1862 as a fireman second class and was promoted to fireman first class. He was discharged on November 30, 1864, at the end of his service. Most of the sailors of the *Alabama* were saved by the *Kearsarge* crew, but Semmes had help from a British vessel and escaped.

In Newburyport, a sister ship (one with the same exact design plan) to the USS *Kearsarge* was built. After the war began and the risk of shipping had increased, George W. Jackman Jr. put in for a government contract and began building a ship to be christened the USS *Marblehead*. It was ready on Wednesday, October 16, 1861. At first, it was found to be stuck due to the heavy machinery, but soon it glided into the Merrimack River.

The occasion was the event of the season, and crowds gathered wherever they could. Mr. Moses Little ran a shuttle from the post office to the spot where people went to watch, Brown's Wharf (currently the area behind the Firehouse Center for the Arts). The 691-ton Unadilla-class screw steam gunboat wasn't christened until March 1862. Its commander was Lieutenant Commander Sommerville Nicholson.

The *Marblehead* did able service as part of McClellan's Peninsula Campaign in 1862. On May 1, it bombarded Yorktown as McClellan made plans to march up to Richmond. It then became part of the naval blockade along the coasts of Georgia and South Carolina. In February 1863, the *Passaic* and the *Marblehead* took a trek up the Wilmington River in Georgia in search of the CSS *Atlanta*, an ironclad that had formerly been the *Fingal*, but without luck. Then followed a few captures of some blockade runners—*Glide*, *Caswell* and *Arago*—and the hauling in of cotton and other goods from them. In the summer of 1863, it participated in conflicts while on the Stono River, South Carolina, attacking Fort Wagner and Charleston Harbor.

It was Christmas Day 1863, though, when it took its place in Civil War history. The *Marblehead* and the *Pawnee* were attacked by Rebels. Three men of the *Marblehead* crew would go on to receive the Medal of Honor. While on the Stono River in South Carolina, not far from Legareville, a battle ensued. The *Marblehead* attacked Confederates on Johns Island, and Boatswain's Mate William Farley, USN, encouraged his men to keep up a rapid fire.

Built in Newburyport, the USS *Marblehead* served the U.S. Navy as part of the blockade of Southern ports, as well as armed engagements on the Stono River and at Fort Wagner. *NHC.*

Then twenty-six-year-old quartermaster James Miller, USN, continued to take soundings while under fire. (Soundings were depth measurements made with a line in the days before sonar, to make sure that the water would carry the ship without running aground.) The third recipient was a man from Virginia who served on the *Marblehead*. He was an ex-slave named Robert Blake. Blake had joined up when the *Marblehead* was in Virginia. Now as a crew member, Blake serviced a rifled gun and carried out his duties, which helped the *Marblehead* force the Rebels from their position and leave behind a caisson and a big gun, along with ammunition.

After that, the *Marblehead* went north for repairs—it had been hit twenty times in the battle—and then served its country as a training ship for the U.S. Naval Academy, which was temporarily located in Newport, Rhode Island.

Three men from Newburyport served on the *Marblehead*. Joseph C. Batchelder was born on October 7, 1835, and served on board. He died in Chelsea, Massachusetts, on April 4, 1890, but was buried in Newburyport. Two other men were born in the Clipper City, but by adulthood they were elsewhere and enlisted as such. Edward F. Ballow lived in Roxbury and enlisted from Boston. He was born in Newburyport on July 1, 1838. He served as fireman second class on the *Marblehead*.

The crew of the USS *Marblehead* produced three Medal of Honor recipients from the engagement on the Stono River in South Carolina. *NHC.*

Boston was home to another man born in Newburyport who served on the USS *Marblehead*. Moses R. Johnson, a painter, was twenty-six years old when he joined the crew but was credited to Fitchburg. Moses left his wife, Jane, and baby daughter, Marion, behind as he went off to serve. He was discharged in January 1864, soon after the *Marblehead* left its mark on history. He returned to Boston and his wife and enlarged his family to include two more daughters, Carrie and Lottie. He took on work as a furniture worker.

George W. Jackman Jr.—the Newburyport man born on Broadway in New York City, as his parents were visiting friends when his mother gave birth—would go on to build other ships for the U.S. Navy, including the *Ascutney*, which was launched on April 4, 1863, and sent to the New York City Navy Yard.

In July, the USS *Ascutney* was put in service, with Lieutenant Commander William Mitchell leading its crew. It sought Confederates in the Gulf of St. Lawrence near Quebec, Nova Scotia and New Brunswick. It also served as part of the blockade of the Southern ports off North Carolina. After a chase of the *Tallahassee* during which the *Ascutney* ran into engine trouble, it was sent to the Washington Navy Yard. In September 1864, it was decommissioned.

Jackman continued to build ships for much of the second half of the nineteenth century. He married a second time—this woman, Rosalie, being twenty years his junior—but he remained on Woodland Street. The couple had a daughter, also named Rosalie, born about a year after the war's end. Jackman died on January 4, 1895, at the age of eighty. His death earned front-page status in the *Newburyport Daily Herald* the next day.

Chapter 7

Citizen Soldiers

BROTHERS-IN-LAW IN ARMS

The war, of course, was fought and won by the common foot soldier. Notably, it was the volunteer who felt a patriotic sense of duty and so signed his name. Here are a few of those local men, most still boys, who did just that.

The lower end of Bromfield Street presented Newburyport with a couple of young volunteers in Thomas E. Cutter and Amos Pettingell. Cutter was born on March 28, 1836, to city alderman Thomas H. and Elizabeth B. (Moody) Cutter. When the war began, he was a twenty-five-year-old house painter at his father's business on 44 Merrimac Street. He was living with his wife's family at 10 Bromfield Street, which is now renumbered 16–18 Bromfield Street.

In 1862, with the formation of the Thirty-fifth Massachusetts Regiment by Albert W. Bartlett, young Mr. Cutter signed up as a corporal of Company B, Thirty-fifth Massachusetts, on August 11, 1862. When he left for war, twenty-six-year-old Thomas left his wife and newborn daughter, Etta, behind. He was with the regiment for the whole war, and soon after enlisting, he was in fierce fighting at places like South Mountain and Antietam. Thomas Cutter was promoted to sergeant on November 1, and by New Year's Day, he was quartermaster sergeant.

During the Kentucky and Mississippi campaigns, Cutter was promoted to first lieutenant on April 1, 1864. He continued as quartermaster through the war and marched in the Grand Review in Washington, D.C. He was discharged and able to return to Newburyport on June 9, 1865.

When the Thirty-fifth Massachusetts, Company B, was formed up, the men marched through the streets of Newburyport, with Mayor Jackman in the lead. This photo is highly likely to be from that time, as the man in front looks like Jackman, and the officer along the side has similar features to Albert W. Bartlett. The uniforms are too fresh to be veterans, and veterans likely wouldn't have muskets, let alone bayonets fixed on them. *HSON.*

After the war, he took on a change in professions and began working in a hat factory. He joined the Grand Army of the Republic (GAR), attending Post No. 49 in Newburyport. He died on May 5, 1903, at the age of sixty-seven and was laid to rest at Oak Hill Cemetery next to his wife, Harriet M. (Pettingell) Cutter.

Thomas Cutter's neighbor and brother-in-law, Amos Pettingell, resided at 8 Bromfield Street, now 12 Bromfield Street. Amos had a home with his wife, Frances, six-year-old daughter, Louisa, and a baby daughter, Alice. Likely the two men went down the same day along with some other friends and fell in with the Thirty-fifth Regiment.

Amos was employed in Newburyport as a cooper (a barrel maker) and would earn the rank of corporal. However, Mr. Pettingell didn't serve long, as he lost a finger at the Battle of South Mountain on September 14. He

The graves of Thomas E. Cutter and his wife, Harriet, at Oak Hill Cemetery. *WH.*

was discharged on November 30 and returned home. He found work in concrete but wouldn't reside in Newburyport forever, as he died in San Diego, California, on January 21, 1898.

AMOS W. LEE ON LAND AND SEA

Another 'Porter who joined, but wasn't from Bromfield Street, was Amos W. Lee. Lee was a mariner by trade, living at 1 Salem Street when the war began.

Lee witnessed big events in the war. When the Thirty-fifth Massachusetts was at Burnside's Bridge at Antietam, he witnessed the body of Albert W. Bartlett on the ambulance as it went by him. He witnessed all of the officers' deaths at the engagement, and he was personally wounded at the famous bridge as well.

Lee was eventually taken to Baltimore for hospitalization. While in the hospital, he saw unimaginable sights. He recalled afterward watching drunken surgeons amputating the wrong arm of a soldier. These "doctors" had little more than one year of college and were allowed to practice their medicine on the wounded heroes.

One day, he awoke in his bed in the ward. A most pungent odor was wafting his way, and he began looking in either direction to see if one of his fellow patients had finally cashed in. Most were sleeping, making the determination more difficult. Then it became evident what the smell was. A few beds down from him, a German immigrant serving his new country had some Limburger cheese under his bed.

Another day, a group of young ladies came to visit the soldiers. The sight of the women pleased the men, and the idea of the contents of the cloth-covered baskets they carried intrigued them even more. Could it be breads? Maybe jellies? How about cakes? The ladies conversed with the men, asking them where they were from, what their home was like and what regiment they served in.

Amos couldn't take it for very long. The army food had been awful, and the thought of what lay undisclosed inside the baskets was too much. Finally,

The monument to the Thirty-fifth Massachusetts was placed near the location where Captain Albert W. Bartlett was killed in action. *MB.*

the women presented their true reason for the visit. They offered the men the items they had brought with them: religious tracts. The women were seeking to spread the gospel.

Amos was discharged due to his injury on November 3, 1862, and made his way back to Newburyport. After some rest, one day he thought he'd head into town. It had been three months since his return, and Amos walked into a drugstore and weighed himself. He weighed a mere sixty-three pounds—a skeleton. His home was 10 Prospect Street (now the parking lot for the Institution for Savings).

Events did not end there. Amos was ready to return to work as a mariner. It was a popular profession in Newburyport. In May 1863, Amos found work on the *Kossuth*, which made business trips to New York City and back to Portsmouth, New Hampshire. One of the items in its hold was malt for the Frank Jones Brewery in Portsmouth.

The Confederate states were the first to institute a draft or conscription, but it wasn't long before the Federal government did the same. The draft was unpopular for many reasons. For one, it was considered cowardly for a man not to join on his own, but the ones currently serving felt that the draftees wouldn't fight. One stipulation to the draft for Uncle Sam was the ability to pay for a substitute. Usually for $300, any man drafted could buy someone to serve in his place. This was trouble for some, who were calling the conflict a "rich man's war."

In the big cities, where immigrants were arriving constantly, hoping to follow their American dreams, the idea of fighting to free the slaves, who could then easily come and take the low-wage, menial jobs that they were getting, didn't sit well either.

Days after the Battle of Gettysburg, New York City erupted over this issue. Many of the Irish and other low-wage earners started what became known as the New York Draft Riots. Other cities had riots over the matter, including Portsmouth, New Hampshire, but New York's is the most famous. Fires were set, looting was rampant and homes were vandalized—and much worse. African Americans who were free and living in New York were lynched in the middle of the city. Sometimes they were also set afire.

By chance, the *Kossuth*, with Amos W. Lee, was in New York doing trade, and Lee saw firsthand the ravages that mankind could inflict on itself. He sat on the deck and was able to see very easily the violence and the destruction that an angry mob can impose. It was something that he never forgot.

Ships known to be owned by Radical Republicans, abolitionists and such were targeted by the mobs looking to vent their anger. Lee recalled how, fortunately, the *Kossuth* was registered in New York and not Massachusetts, as the mob in New York probably would have rampaged through the ship he was on if not.

After the second day of riots, the captain decided to leave New York, even though the cargo hold was only about half full. Too much danger and risk left the crew nervous, and the safety of the water was much better.

On their way out, they were accosted by a troop transport whose crew told the captain that they needed to use his ship to go back to New York. The captain complained and told them that he was moving out with the tide and could not. The troops found other means. President Lincoln eventually sent troops, fresh from Gettysburg, to quell the melee with Pennsylvania and Maryland troops and set New York back on track.

Amos W. Lee continued working on ships. With ill health, a friend suggested that he join a ship off the South Carolina and Georgia coasts helping to move military supplies. Perhaps the warmer climate would do him some good. Lee's health was not the best, and he suffered from fever on more than one occasion.

The region was fairly safe but for some torpedoes from the Rebels. Torpedoes during this time in history were more like mines. Lee described an African American on a small boat going out to move a log, unaware that a line was connected to the log. The poor man went well into the air.

In April 1865, the ship Lee was on was headed to Florida but was delayed. Lee was witness to the flag-raising over Fort Sumter four years after it was taken down.

John Black: Newburyport's First Loss

Many men made their living on the water here in Newburyport. The Black family on School Street was one such group. John Black resided on School Street with his wife, Maria, from Nova Scotia. They had two children at the outset of the war: Ellen, five, and John, three.

The house must have been a full one, as twelve people called it home. Not only was John's family there, but his three brothers—George, James and William—also resided under the same roof. All four brothers worked as seamen in the port of Newburyport.

As the war began, other people were living at this home in the neighborhood of the birthplace of William Lloyd Garrison. They consisted

John Black died in Newburyport in 1862 just a short time after coming home from service. He was buried at New Hill Cemetery. *WH.*

of the Ryan family: Mary, forty-six; Hollis, twenty-nine; and Hanson, twenty-five. Two more people in the house included another woman from Nova Scotia, Catherine McGrader, and Mainer Angeline Boker. The Ryans were shoemakers, and the others worked in the mills.

After it became clear that the war was showing no sign of a quick and early end, other regiments were formed. One of these was the Eleventh Massachusetts, Company C. This was Luther Dame's group. John Black enlisted and was mustered in on November 18, 1861, as a private.

It was to be a three-year enlistment, but Black's course ended quickly. While in the Army of the Potomac, Private John Black fought in Yorktown, Williamsburg, Fair Oaks, Glendale and Malvern Hill. What hit him, though, was not lead, but rather the one enemy that struck more soldiers on both sides than any other: disease. He was discharged because of disability on August 15, 1862, with typhoid fever. He only lasted two more weeks.

John Black holds the distinction of having had the first military funeral from the Civil War in Newburyport. On the day he died, Friday, August 29, the city made plans for Newburyport's distinguished son. Funeral services were held at his home. The procession then made its way to New Hill Cemetery. More words were said, and John Black was laid to rest. His widow and children would not be left alone for too long. John's brother, George, married Maria and raised the family as his own, having never had any children.

George served in the navy during the Civil War on ships *J.P. Jackson, Potomac* and *Monongahela*. He was near Admiral David Farragut during the Battle of New Orleans, and he was involved in the attack on Vicksburg on the Mississippi. He was discharged on April 15, 1865, the day Lincoln died.

For thirty years, he worked for the Newburyport Fire Department at Engine No. 2. He outlived Maria and died on August 1908 at the age of seventy-one.

Joseph Barlow: From First Shots to Final Shots

Among the first men to leave Newburyport on that cold April day in 1861 was Joseph Barlow.

When the war began, twenty-seven-year-old Joseph Barlow and his Irish wife, Ellen, had two young daughters, three and one and a half years old. Barlow worked as a shoemaker and, of course, was involved in the Cushing Guards.

Barlow was with the Eighth Massachusetts for those first ninety days. He was there each and every step through Annapolis, Washington and Baltimore and came home to that celebration on August 1, 1861. However, Joseph didn't sit still, and he enlisted in the Twenty-third Massachusetts Regiment, Company I, that September. This was a three-year deal, and Barlow was ready to do his patriotic duty.

The Twenty-third Massachusetts followed Burnside through North Carolina as part of the XVIII Corps. Barlow participated in battles at Roanoke Island, New Berne, Kingston and Whitehall in 1862. He became a corporal and then a sergeant by the end of 1863. Before his promotion in 1865 to second lieutenant, he also fought at Drury's Bluff, was part of the capture of City Point, the Bermuda Hundred and Cold Harbor and then was part of the first assault on Petersburg. He was mustered out as second lieutenant at the war's end. He was discharged on June 25, 1865.

Joseph's younger brother, Franklin, also served in the war, but he was credited to Lowell.

After the war, Joseph Barlow resumed his profession making shoes and joined the GAR. He and his wife had increased their family to include five children by 1870, four girls and a middle boy. More children would arrive before the end of the century as the Barlow family lived on Atwood Street.

Only a few men could claim that they were there to answer the call for volunteers and left one day after the request. Joseph Barlow was one. *WH.*

53

FOLLOWING IN HIS FATHER'S FOOTSTEPS

Albert W. Bartlett's recruiting job in 1862 produced Company B of the Thirty-fifth Massachusetts Regiment.

The men left town in August, and one of the soon-to-be-notable soldiers was George William Creasey, who had just celebrated his twenty-second birthday in June. George was a shoemaker like his father, George Creasey, who was one of the first men to leave Newburyport to defend the Union.

Within a few weeks, this regiment, which functioned under the command of Ambrose Burnside's IX Corps of the Army of the Potomac, would fight in prominent battles such as at South Mountain and Antietam, where Captain Bartlett was killed in action. George W. Creasey continued with the regiment. After all, he had signed up for three years, and there was a lot of war on the horizon. Creasey fought at Sulphur Springs that November 15 and was involved in the Union devastation at Fredericksburg, Virginia, on December 13, 1862. However, the Thirty-fifth Massachusetts kept moving.

In February 1863, the Thirty-fifth Massachusetts was sent to Newport News, Virginia, but only briefly, and soon it was with General Grant as he persisted with his attacks on Vicksburg, Mississippi. In May, Creasey was promoted to first lieutenant. Creasey and the Thirty-fifth were with Grant on July 4, when Vicksburg fell and the Union marched into town. This victory put complete control of the Mississippi River in the hands of the Union. This was followed by action at Jackson, Mississippi, and yet another victory with General Grant.

That autumn, George was an ordnance officer in Knoxville, Tennessee, and by January 1864, he was commander of the barracks at Covington, Kentucky. He was detailed by Brigade Commander General Sumner Carruth, another Massachusetts man, as assistant adjutant in April 1864. George was back in combat within days of his new position, as he was part of the Battle of the Wilderness on May 6. This was followed by action at Spotsylvania and North Anna River, where he was captured and taken as a prisoner of war.

The notorious Libby prison in Richmond was his next stop. After he was confined here for a time, he was sent to Macon and Savannah, Georgia, and then to a jail in Charleston, South Carolina, where he was under fire. He was moved to Columbia, South Carolina, and then to North Carolina, where he was paroled and came through the lines near Wilmington on March 1, 1865.

After surrender and the war's end, but before returning to Newburyport, George W. Creasey had the honor of being part of the Grand Review, during which regiment after regiment and officer and officer proudly marched the streets of Washington to be reviewed by President Andrew Johnson and other dignitaries.

George W. Creasey spent a good part of the remainder of his life working on veterans' causes. Along with fifteen other men, he applied for the charter in 1868 for Newburyport's Grand Army of the Republic, Post No. 49.

For most of the remainder of his life, Creasey lived with his wife Sarah's family at 37 Temple Street. His wife just happened to be the sister of the late Albert W. Bartlett, the leader of the first men to leave at the request of President Lincoln.

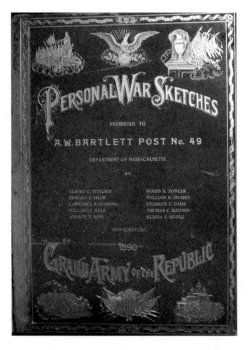

When writing his book, Creasey relied heavily on Post No. 49's "Personal War Sketches." The GAR post had this oversized book from 1890. In it, many members had their personal war histories handwritten, including each engagement, where they served and when they were discharged. Special thanks to Scott Nason. *WH.*

Creasey undertook one more monumental task; it had to occupy a large amount of his time, but on the other hand, it had to be a labor of love as well. Realizing that the men were aging and that many of their experiences needed recording for history, he compiled and wrote *The City of Newburyport in the Civil War 1861–65*, published in 1903.

George William Creasey died on July 3, 1909.

JOSEPH L. JOHNSON: THREE DIFFERENT REGIMENTS

Joseph Lawrence Johnson was born on November 27, 1829, in Newburyport to parents Samuel L. and Martha H. Johnson. Born and raised in Newburyport, Joseph made his living as a furniture dealer to support both himself and his wife, Harriet. He did what most men did and joined the local militia, the Cushing Guards.

When the call by Albert W. Bartlett went out in April 1861, Johnson was among the first men to leave town with Company A of the Eighth Massachusetts. He was in service in Annapolis and Washington and then guarded the Baltimore and Ohio Railroad before returning to Clipper City on August 1, 1861.

Like many of the men who came home, his service to his home and country did not end there. On September 15, 1862, after being home for one year, he left Newburyport as a first lieutenant, again with the Cushing Guards. His second time in service had him serving garrison duty from December 1862 to July 1863 at Fort Parke, Roanoke Island, North Carolina.

Johnson and some other men from this regiment volunteered to serve for a brief time in July 1863 at Maryland Heights, a strategic location in Maryland overlooking Harpers Ferry. He was discharged on August 7, but his service was not yet finished.

The Sixtieth Regiment, Massachusetts Volunteer Militia, Company H, was needed in Indianapolis to guard Confederate prisoners of war. Joseph L. Johnson was again a first lieutenant with this group of men obliged to serve for one hundred days. He finally finished his service on August 1, 1864, returned home, became a house carpenter and eventually lived with his father-in-law, Henry Stockman. Joseph lived out his days until December 5, 1898. He was buried at Oak Hill Cemetery.

JAMES P.L. WESTCOTT AND THE MOZART REGIMENT

Within days of Albert W. Bartlett's Cushing Guards leaving Newburyport, the idea of a new company of men was suggested, to be called the Newburyport National Guards.

Captain of the National Guards was thirty-seven-year-old James P.L. Westcott. On May 13, 1861, he sent word to the governor that they were ready to join the Eighth Regiment. He sent a second telegram the same day, saying that his men were "crazy to go." On May 23, 1861, they traveled to Boston to be reviewed by Governor John Andrew. There were about seventy men in the ranks, not counting the band that accompanied them.

The governor formed six more regiments for the state via General Order No. 12. Each was to be full of three-year men. The Honorable Eben F. Stone and Captain Westcott visited the governor to see where the new regiment might fit in. They were reassured that these men would be brought into one of the new regiments the governor had requested.

Instead, Captain Westcott received the following on May 29, 1861, from Governor John A. Andrew: "If you can be in Brooklyn, N.Y., Saturday morning, you can be received into the Brooklyn Phalanx and go into active service immediately."[13] Captain Nehemiah Flanders had trained these men. Flanders had been a key member of the Cushing Guards before resigning, allowing Bartlett to command.

The men left on Friday, May 31, 1861. Captain Westcott left his wife, Susan, and eight-year-old son, George, to defend his country. His daughter, Katherine Cook, was twenty-two and left at home as well. When the patriotic departure took place, cheers and speeches were made, including a rousing monologue by Caleb Cushing in defense of the flag.

At this time in history, states often saw themselves as independent units, and when the Massachusetts men arrived, some wanted to return them. Westcott argued, and finally the Newburyport National Guards, as well as some other regiments from Massachusetts, were allowed to join the newly formed Fortieth New York Regiment (Mozart Regiment). Neighbors also joined the Mozart men as the Wallace Guards of Amesbury fell in.

By becoming the Fortieth New York, this severed their connections to Massachusetts, meaning that the men's actions would now reflect on New York and that Massachusetts took no responsibility for them or their welfare.

The Mozart Regiment was a truly motley group. Newburyport's men were Company B, Milford's were Company G, Company H was from West Cambridge and K was from Lawrence. Two companies were from Pennsylvania. They were mustered into service on July 1, 1861, in Yonkers. The name came from Mozart Hall. They left New York on July 4.

These men fought valiantly and participated in such battles as Fair Oaks, Seven Days, Second Bull Run, Fredericksburg, Chancellorsville, Gettysburg, the Wilderness, Cold Harbor and the Siege of Petersburg. At Gettysburg, they were in position in a wood near the Wheatfield and, in the course of action, were the extreme left of the army, outnumbered three to one and in the Devil's Den. They held off Hood's Confederates long enough for the reinforcements of the Union to occupy Little Round Top. They were also part of the Appomattox campaign that led to Lee's surrender.

James P.L. Westcott had been in shipbuilding. He had led a strike in the 1850s that blacklisted him for many things. Still, by 1857, he had secured a job as police marshal, although Jonathan Kennison managed to start a petition to remove Westcott. In January 1860, the mayor had to go against the wishes of many citizens who wanted to eliminate the marshal position altogether. Westcott was not liked by many, but the friction between those people and Westcott subsided when he entered the war.

After the war, he resumed duties as police marshal. The *Herald* reported on March 10, 1866, that a large robbery (worth $1.5 million) had taken place in New York. Westcott caught the thief, as he was in New York at the time, and received a reward of $25,000.

Westcott died on February 1900 at his home on Spring Street at the age of seventy-five.

A SCHOOLTEACHER VOLUNTEERS

If ever there was a man who epitomized the well-rounded gentleman of the nineteenth century, it was Luther Dame. Joseph and Statira Dame's son was born in Kittery, Maine, on March 3, 1826. Although from Maine, Luther left his mark on Newburyport more than any other place.

At the age of nineteen, he was a teacher at the "Old Red School" of the Old Green. Through a series of letters of recommendation, Luther Dame came to teach at the Putnam Free School. This was the high school at the corner of High and Green Streets where the current Catholic school is. He taught mathematics and French.

In the 1850s, just a short time before the Civil War, there was another kind of civil war brewing in one of the United States' territories, Kansas. For years, the peace had been kept between North and South through the Missouri Compromise of 1820. That law kept a balance of free and slave states. Usually, a pair would be admitted to the Union at the same time, one North (free) and one South (slave).

The Kansas-Nebraska Act changed all of that. This piece of legislation meant that the people of a particular territory would vote for the side they deemed best suited for them. Abolitionists were discouraged by this new law. William Lloyd Garrison wrote regarding this law, "The deed is done—the slave power is again victorious."[14]

Parties from both the North and the South converged on Kansas with the hopes of influencing the population and settling Kansas with people of their persuasion. Men came in from Missouri to influence the population and push Kansas to be a slave state. These men were known as "Border Ruffians." A number of people from Massachusetts also went to Kansas, their goal being to sway the votes to stop the expansion of slavery into yet another state. Luther Dame was among those who went in with an abolitionist frame of mind.

Luther Dame had been in Kansas to help its statehood under Governor Robinson. Dame surveyed land and helped set up Topeka as the capital. Some of Newburyport's sons and daughters settled there, calling it home. While in Kansas, Dame met John Brown, a zealot willing to end slavery under any circumstance and by any means.

Two events in 1856 changed Kansas. The first was the attack by proslavery forces on Lawrence, where they looted the town, burned buildings and destroyed two printing presses. The next day, Massachusetts senator Charles Sumner was beaten within an inch of his life on the Senate floor by Congressman Preston Brooks of South Carolina after Sumner gave an antislavery speech. John Brown retaliated with his own attacks, and thus began the series of events known to history as "Bleeding Kansas."

Sources don't put Luther Dame in the Kansas violence. He returned to Massachusetts and by 1860 was living in Nahant with his wife, Sarah, and the first two children of seven he and Sarah would have. Luther returned to work as a schoolteacher.

In January 1863, Luther Dame's brother bought for him the former J.A. McArthur studios, and Luther Dame added photography to his credits. His reputation as a photographer was well known into the twentieth century. *NPLAC.*

As the Civil War began for the whole country, Luther Dame found himself in the fall of 1861 mustered in as captain of the Eleventh Massachusetts, Company C, Massachusetts Volunteer Militia. These men were also called the McClellan Guards. With these men, Dame saw action in skirmishes before Yorktown and Williamsburg. He was at the siege of Yorktown on April 5 and at the Battle of Williamsburg on May 5, 1862.

On May 15, he resigned his commission and returned home. However, his service was nowhere near complete. He next organized the Newburyport City Cadets on September 1, 1863, and was elected captain. In May 1864, he was mustered in as captain of the Third Unattached Company, Massachusetts Infantry. These were the City Cadets. This was to be a three-month service, and the men were not to be far from home since they were stationed in Salem Harbor at Forts Lee and Pickering in Salem, Massachusetts. He was discharged at the end of the term on August 5, 1864.

The next project for Luther Dame was to recruit a company to be posted at Fort Nichols, by the mouth of the Merrimack River (in the area now known as the Salisbury Beach State Reservation) on the Salisbury side.

The multitalented citizen Luther Dame was laid to rest in 1913. His second wife, Josephine H. (Noyes) Dame, joined him in 1934. *WH.*

Before this bunch of men was mustered, however, the war ended, and they were sent home.

The remarkable story of Luther Dame continued even after the war. Luther became the first commander of the Newburyport Grand Army of the Republic, Post No. 49. He continued to fight for veterans' causes and appear at veterans' ceremonies and events.

For twenty years, Luther taught at Newburyport High School after the school board condensed the high schools in town. Science was his interest. He was a civil engineer; had a photography business; served in the Massachusetts House of Representatives, the state senate and the local board of aldermen; was president of the Anna Jacques Hospital Association, president of the Newburyport Cooperative Bank and cofounder of the Historic Society of Old Newbury; was a Mason; and participated in various celebrations and occasions for Newburyport.

In 1893, Sarah died. Soon after, in 1896, Luther sold property at 13 Otis Place and moved to San Diego with family. But California must not have sat well with him because in February 1899, the *Daily News* reported that he had sold his San Diego property and was moving back to Newburyport.

Luther continued to be part of veterans' reunions and causes. It was reported on June 26, 1903, that he along with six other Newburyport men would attend the General Joseph Hooker parade in Boston.

Somewhere in the midst of this, he remarried. Luther Dame, a descendant of Aquila Chase, one of Newbury's first settlers, married Josephine H. Noyes, herself descended from one of the first settlers, Nicholas Noyes.

They lived at what is now 78 Purchase Street until Luther's death on May 15, 1913. Josephine lived until 1934. Both of Luther's wives are buried near him along the fence to March's Hill at Oak Hill Cemetery.

THE NOYES BROTHERS

Many names throughout this book can be traced to the first settlers of Newbury. In 1635, the first Europeans landed and made a settlement here and, over the years, played their roles in the history of the colonies and the country.

One such name on the roster is Noyes. Timothy K. and Sarah Noyes had eleven children, not an uncommon thing for the early nineteenth century. Three of their eight sons—Joseph H.W. Noyes, Ebenezer Noyes and George

S. Noyes—all served. Their oldest son, William, and his wife, Frances Noyes, had a son, Charles, who served as well.

At what would be considered an old age to join as a soldier, shoemaker Joseph enlisted in Company H of the Sixtieth Massachusetts. He was forty-one years old when he signed up on July 19, 1864, and then mustered in four days later. This was a one-hundred-day enlistment, and Joseph was sent to Indianapolis, Indiana, to guard Confederate POWs in the camp there. He returned to his home on Marlboro Street after his discharge on November 30 of that year.

Younger brother Ebenezer Noyes signed up earlier in the war than big brother Joseph. Eben joined the Cushing Guards on August 11, 1862, and was mustered in on September 15, 1862, just two days after his twenty-fifth birthday.

Ebenezer was born in Newbury, unlike big brother Joseph, who was born in Seabrook, New Hampshire. Still, this young millworker grew up in Newburyport and signed up to do his part. He was a corporal in Company A of the Eighth Massachusetts for a nine-month stint. From December 4, 1862, to July 12, 1863, he was stationed at Fort Park, Roanoke Island, North Carolina, with his job as garrison duty. He was discharged on August 7, 1863, and it wasn't too long before he reenlisted. This time he was with brother Joseph in the Sixtieth MVM, with the rank of sergeant. As with his brother, this was only a one-hundred-day service, and Ebenezer came home to Newburyport before moving out to the Worcester area for the remainder of his life. He called Northbridge home, but when he died on July 15, 1886, his remains were taken to Noyes Hill in Oak Hill Cemetery, where he joined other family members.

George S. Noyes was born in Newbury and called Newburyport home. George followed brother Ebenezer to the Cushing Guards and enlisted on August 11, 1862, one day after his twentieth birthday. George was also at Fort Park with his brother. He was discharged on August 7, 1863. He, too, decided to reenlist and joined the Sixtieth Massachusetts guarding Rebel prisoners. But when those one hundred days were up, he went yet again, and this time joined the Sixty-second Massachusetts Company D as a corporal on March 23, 1865. This was a short-lived term, as the war ended soon. For this last enlistment, Salem got the credit for George S. Noyes. In May 1865, he was discharged and returned to his job as a shoemaker and to his home with his wife Abby on Lime Street, Newburyport. He died in February 1885 as a resident of Milk Street.

Joseph, Ebenezer and George had a nephew, Charles S. Noyes, who joined the Third Unattached Company, Massachusetts Infantry, for ninety days. He was garrisoned at Fort Lee and Fort Pickering in Salem Harbor.

Fort Pickering in Salem Harbor became home to many young men from Newburyport. *HSQN.*

His term expired in August 1864. Charles was nineteen years old when he served. Charles would live on Lunt Street and raise a family with his wife, Caroline, and later they moved to what is now 58 Milk Street. He drove a bread cart in town. Charles lived well into the next century and died on October 12, 1932, at eighty-seven.

The only men of this family to join the GAR Post No. 49 were George and Charles. Charles would at one point hold the job as post commander.

Joseph, Ebenezer and George had a niece named Josephine, who married Luther Dame.

SARAH E. SMITH: DEVOTED NURSE

Jeremiah Downs Jr. of Newburyport served in the Eleventh Massachusetts. He enlisted in Company D and was mustered in on November 1, 1861. It was a three-year enlistment, but Private Downs was discharged after a year of service for disability. He succumbed to his wounds and died in Roxbury in February 1863. His family had him buried in Newburyport.

Sarah, Jeremiah Jr. and George Downs were the children of Jeremiah and Abigail Downs of Newburyport. However, Sarah holds the distinction of doing something during the Civil War that no other woman from

Newburyport did: she volunteered her services as a nurse. Before the Civil War, nursing was not considered a job for a lady. Those who were taken in as nurses had to be married. However, by the end of the war, they took anyone they could.

Sarah E. Smith began her nursing in early 1862. Her husband, George, had died in 1854 in Lahaina, St. Thomas. So, at thirty-two years old, an age considered safe for nursing, she was accepted by the people running the hospitals. She felt the need to help in some way, and now she could.

Sarah soon became the matron of Trinity Church Hospital in Washington, located in Georgetown just on the edge of the nation's capital. Like the famous Clara Barton, Sarah didn't contain her tasks to the hospital, as she often ventured out to the battlefields to help wounded men in the Army of the Potomac.

Unfortunately for Sarah, she contracted an illness. It was enough to force her back home. It transformed into consumption (known as tuberculosis today). Many men from Massachusetts and others, especially from Pennsylvania, would not forget her.

Newburyport's famous Civil War nurse, Sarah E. Smith, suffered from illness before succumbing to the effects at the age of forty-two. She was buried at New Hill Cemetery. *WH.*

Sarah moved in with her brother, George W. Downs, who was now living in Boston and working as a painter. Their mother, Abby, lived with them, too. Sarah's affliction kept her confined to the home, but all those who knew her said that she was always in good spirits.

Sarah lived a few more years, suffering through her illness and finally passing away on January 2, 1873, at the age of forty-two. Her last wishes were to be buried under the auspices of the Grand Army of the Republic. Her funeral was held at the Pleasant Street Church in Newburyport, and she was laid to rest at New Hill, also known as Highland Cemetery, next to her brother Jeremiah Jr. Later, in 1892, George joined them both.

JOSEPH E. MOODY AND ANOTHER NEWBURYPORT

To say that soldiers are brothers in arms is no small matter. Living under and experiencing the most horrendous events together bonds men like nothing else possibly could.

Joseph Edward Moody had just turned twenty years old when the Civil War began that frightful April 1861. His home during the war years was listed as 7 Milk Street. He joined the Forty-eighth Massachusetts, Company A, a nine-month unit, enlisting on August 9, 1862, He was mustered in as corporal on September 16. By the following September, when he was discharged at the end of the term of service, he had been promoted to sergeant major and had participated in a variety of battles in the Louisiana Gulf area, such as Plain's Store, Port Hudson and Donaldsonville.

After a break back in Newburyport, Joseph reenlisted. This time, he joined a veteran regiment. These men had served before. The Fifty-ninth Massachusetts recruited at the end of 1863 and into the early part of 1864. On March 29, 1864, he was commissioned a second lieutenant of the three-year regiment.

This band was part of the IX Corps in the Army of the Potomac. Lieutenant Moody saw action in the Wilderness on May 6; at Spotsylvania, Virginia, on May 12 and 18; and at the North Anna River on May 24. Not long after Cold Harbor, Virginia, on June 2, he was taken as a prisoner of war.

Mosby's guerrillas were the men taking him to Libby Prison in Richmond, Virginia. Moody had twenty-five dollars on him and hid the twenty-dollar bill in his mouth so if the Confederates found the five, they might think that's

One of the infamous Civil War prisons was Libby Prison in Richmond, Virginia. Joseph E. Moody described the horrors that faced any man taken to Libby. Note the whitewashed lower floor. *LOC.*

all he had. Mosby's men stripped him of his gear and uniform and gave him some homespun, ill-fitting rags.

Libby Prison was an old warehouse converted into a prison. The exterior walls were whitewashed on the ground floors to make nighttime escapes difficult without being seen. Inside, Moody described the rooms as small and dark, with low ceilings. Prisoners who didn't behave themselves would be sent into the basement, where a room eight feet by eight feet was waiting for them. It only had a one-foot-square opening in the ceiling—enough to drop in some food and water twice a day. The gloomy conditions allowed the only other inhabitants, rats, a perfect home. Rats were all around, and at night, prisoners had to beat them with sticks to defend themselves.

When he arrived, Moody was taken to the office and "encountered a stern dark complexioned man." This was Dick Turner, the keeper of Libby Prison.[15] After getting Lieutenant Moody's name and age, he asked if he had any money. By now, Moody had sewn the twenty dollars into his clothes. It was swiftly found. He was also shoved against the wall and was measured against it. He realized afterward that this was for making a coffin.

Afterward, he was a prisoner proper. He looked at his surroundings and saw men in bunches, some alone and all in various positions of standing, sitting or lying down. A walk to the window gave him the shock of the reality of the situation: a rifle was aimed right at him. Anyone getting too close to any window would find the same. He found a place that had been vacated by its former resident and made it his, guarding it the best he could.

At five o'clock in the afternoon, a slave boy would enter the room with a basket on his head containing corncakes, one inch thick and five inches square. These were fed to them twice a day. Twice a week, the prisoners received a piece of meat, either beef or pork. It was so tough that one of the fellow prisoners joked that the animal had been killed to save it.

Early on, Moody tried saving some of his food so that he might enjoy some sort of food for breakfast, but upon waking up, he discovered that the rats had walked off with it. Mornings were not a pleasant time. A cart would be brought in to the prison, and men who had died overnight would be hauled out, sometimes as many as thirty to forty men.

At about the end of June, fifty men, including Lieutenant Moody, were placed on a rail car. There was room to stand or sit, but that was it. They received corn bread twice a day, and they were allowed fifteen minutes of fresh air every day. For eight days, they traveled, with the temperature being at least ninety degrees, as the cramped men made their way to Macon, Georgia. The stockade prison in Macon had a stream running through it. Over this stream were pens for the men. Upstream was for drinking and cooking, and the lower end was for washing and sewerage.

It must have been tearful when Moody saw friendly faces at Macon: George W. Creasey, Henry M. Cross, Lieutenant Richard Chute and Captain Hastings. The men formed a "family" and constantly helped one another. Occasionally, Captain John G.B. Adams joined them, and he was always good for cheerfulness.

The food at Macon was not much better. It consisted of a pint of cornmeal daily and a piece of bacon once a week. They did receive a ration of beans, but it contained worms. Before cooking the beans, they would take sticks and remove the worms the best they could. Morale was high, though, and on the Fourth of July, they began a bit of cheerful celebration but were soon ordered by the guard to keep quiet.

At the end of August, when General Sherman was in Georgia, the Rebels took Moody and his comrades out of Macon so as not to be saved by

Standing left: Captain J.G.B. Adams of the Nineteenth Massachusetts. *Standing right*: Captain Henry M. Cross. *Seated, from left*: Lieutenant R.M. Chute, Captain Arthur Monroe and Lieutenant Joseph E. Moody. These men found one another as POWs and helped one another survive unbearable conditions. *NPLAC*.

Sherman. Another train ride ensued, and Lieutenant Moody was on his way to Savannah, Georgia. In Savannah, they were confined to a yard next to a hospital. For forty days, they had better conditions, with fresh meat twice a week, and slept on pine needles at night. It was much healthier overall.

Sherman was on the move, so again the Rebels packed Moody and the other prisoners on the train. Sherman was marching to the sea, so this time Moody and his Newburyport friends were taken to Charleston, South Carolina. They were put in the state prison.

The U.S. Navy was bombarding the city, and the Rebels moved their prisoners in harm's way in retaliation for the attacks on the city. Buildings were set on fire and damaged as fifty to sixty shells per day were lobbed into Charleston, the city where the war had begun.

As winter was approaching, Lieutenant Moody, Lieutenant Chute, Captain Cross and the rest of their "family" were taken to yet another place for detention. This time, it was the yard of the insane asylum. It had a high stockade fence dividing the area, and cracks allowed glimpses. Moody remembered, "On one side the lunatics peeped through at us and on the other side we peeped though at them. No doubt both sides thought the others were crazy."

At one point, they were allowed to go into the local woodlot and chop some trees to make a shelter. The weather was cold now, and shelter and fire were very important. The "family" now consisted of three men from Newburyport, so that name was made and placed over the front as identification.

Bloodhounds were kept by the guards, and one day one managed to get in and walk near Moody. He and the other men knocked it on the head and buried it.

Life was still tough, as scurvy and diarrhea were common and, in some cases, deadly. The lack of proper food and sanitary conditions meant that even life as a prisoner didn't mean a long life.

About this time came a chance to get some of what the men needed. Local businessmen were allowed to conduct some trade with the prisoners. Confederate money was worth about half the U.S. currency. But the prices were still steep. In U.S. money, one dollar bought a loaf of bread, a quart of beans or two turnips. Other food was available for the price as well: beef was six to seven dollars per pound; butter went for fifteen dollars per pound; beans were a bargain at two dollars per quart; potatoes were forty dollars per peck; onions were one dollar each; and molasses was seven dollars per quart.

The new year of 1865 had begun. Lincoln was reelected. Sherman had ripped through Georgia and was coming up to South Carolina. Once again, the "family" was on the move. Joseph E. Moody could see it in soldiers and guards. They saw the writing on the wall and knew that the end was coming. Before leaving their log shelter, they burned it so as to not allow the Rebels the ability to capture "Newburyport."

Once, while on their way to Charlotte, North Carolina, the men were standing in an open field—under guard, of course—and realized that some of their fellow prisoners were running off without being detected. Henry Cross quickly noticed the events and asked, "Who will make an attempt to escape with me?"[16] Some of the men in blue told him that he'd be caught and that it wasn't worth the chance. Cross said that he'd go alone if he had to, and Moody then replied, "I shall go with you!"[17]

Placing some rice in their pockets, they managed to get by the guards without notice. After a quick run to a hole for hiding, they placed some boughs over them for cover and hid until dark. About an hour later, Moody and Cross heard footsteps and saw two Confederate soldiers looking down on them. "Well, Yanks?" Moody replied, "Well, Johnnies, we suppose the jig is up. We'll go back with you."

The Rebels said, "Now, you'uns needn't go back. You're all right to get away."[18] Then the Rebels told Moody and Cross that they were going to head over the hill and that if anyone came this way, they'd tell them that there weren't any Yanks that way.

Once the view was clear, they continued on their move, over a meadow and into a ditch. After a thundershower came upon them, they became tired and wet. They approached a slave cabin and asked for any food they might have. The Newburyporters also hoped that these slaves might be able to help them across the river.

They had some food but were told that it was too close to daylight for trying any sort of crossing. To hide Moody and Cross, they were told to wait in a corn bin. The tired men fell asleep. At about noon, Moody awoke to eyes peering through cracks at him. He nudged Cross, and the two waited to see what would happen next. A voice ordered them to come down the ladder, which they did. It was a squad of Rebels, and they escorted Moody and Cross to a guardhouse for the night.

By chance, an exchange had taken place, and both were allowed to go. They took a train, riding on the roof at the risk of falling off, and were formally exchanged in Wilmington on March 1, a day Joseph E. Moody would always celebrate.

Lieutenant Moody became Mr. Joseph E. Moody, who returned to life on Milk Street. He got a job as a bookkeeper for a time and then got into sales. He became very active in the Newburyport GAR. Joseph married Inez and lived with his mother-in-law, Lois White. Edward was the couple's first son, born in 1868, and Arthur was born at the end of 1870. Joseph Moody's new "family" moved to 147 Water Street. The family then moved to 218 High Street, which is currently 230 High Street. Here he lived out his days and died on October 20, 1916. He was laid to rest at Oak Hill Cemetery.

Chapter 8

Not All Defended the Union

ALBERT PIKE

It's hard to believe that a city like Newburyport, in the northeastern corner of Massachusetts, the most vilified place for proslavery men, could have been the home of a Confederate general. But it was.

A young couple from Byfield, Benjamin and Sarah (Andrews) Pike, were married on June 5, 1808. Sarah was from Ipswich, and Benjamin was a Byfielder. He was a cobbler and had been working in Boston for some time. They had a son, Albert Pike, born on December 29, 1809, in Boston. There are no records of his birth in Boston, probably due to the family connection to Byfield. Not long after Albert was born, the family moved to Byfield and then soon moved again to Newburyport. His father died in 1833, and his mother married Paul Pillsbury.

Albert's uncle, Alfred W. Pike, was a professor at Framingham Academy. Although Benjamin and Sarah had little money, Alfred agreed to tutor Albert to help him get into Harvard. One night, Albert approached his uncle after taking a series of history books to read and asked to be quizzed on their content. The elder Pike didn't think that the young man could retain let alone regurgitate the lessons of these books, but he granted his nephew's wish. At random points within the volumes, Albert had memorized all of the facts pertaining to the books. Alfred knew that his brother's son had a talent.

The uncle and nephew went off to Harvard to put young Albert's skills to the test. While Albert took the entrance exam, Alfred went looking to find someone in Boston who might give them a loan or credit to pay the tuition, which was about $100 per year. There was no money to be found, and although Albert was smart enough, he wouldn't be able to attend Harvard without money.

With the intelligence came conceit and vanity, and Albert felt on every occasion in which a conflict arose that he was right simply by virtue of his knowledge. His ego grew nearly as big as his stout frame, and he was determined to retry at Harvard. His plan was to work, earn some money and make another go of it. He got a job teaching at a common school in Gloucester and lived in a boardinghouse owned by a sea captain. Albert studied all he could at night and saved what money he was able with a plan in mind.

The big, strapping young man was also quite pleased to find two young ladies at the boardinghouse, one being the daughter of the sea captain. Albert, with his assuredness, kept a romantic life all the while focusing on his studies.

The following summer, he returned to Newburyport. Here he continued a lifestyle, to his mother's chagrin, that resembled his father's carefree life of fun. Albert was not content to live a pious life. Throughout his life, he wrote poetry against the wishes of his mother, who considered it frivolous and sinful.

The time came to try Harvard again. He thought that he could enter as a junior and skip the first two years' tuition. Harvard agreed, given his level of intelligence. He had learned on his own in one year what the university would have taught him in two. However, administrators required that he still pay for the first two years. Albert did not have $200 to pay for an education he had already learned.

Albert then came back to Newburyport and began teaching. He also pursued his poetry and published much in Boston, but poetry was not a lucrative endeavor.

The members of the school board in Newburyport did not like the example that Pike was setting for his students. They wanted their teachers to be spotless, and Albert Pike was enjoying his life on his terms. The board tried making him principal, hoping that the responsibility thrust on him would settle him down, but it didn't.

During this time in American history, many people were looking for fortune and fame elsewhere—namely the West. Pike saw this as an opportunity for advancing himself into other realms. He left Newburyport in March 1831 with his friend, Rufus Titcomb, and another named Chase. The young men walked for most of their journey, with the goal being St. Louis and beyond, perhaps to Santa Fe. By the time they reached St.

Louis, Chase, who had been homesick since day one, left his other two friends and returned to Massachusetts.

St. Louis, though, would not be where Albert Pike would settle and make his life. Instead, Arkansas became his home, and here he would become a well-respected man. He married a southern woman, Mary Ann Hamilton from Mississippi, and settled in Fort Smith, Arkansas, where he worked as a schoolteacher and editor of a newspaper. Pike didn't like slavery but saw no other course for the South if agriculture was to be the main way of life. He also was a proponent of the rights of Indians and women.

In the early 1830s, Pike wrote poetry, taught school, studied law and, while representing many of the local tribes, learned many of the languages of the native people. His poetry even impressed another writer of his time, Edgar Allan Poe.

Pike did his part in the Mexican-American War and returned to Arkansas in 1848. From here, he began editorializing for the *Arkansas Gazette* on the subject of the transcontinental railroad. Pike saw the railroad as a way to help the South thrive economically, become more industrial and hopefully encourage the slow transition to ending slavery.

The year 1850 saw Pike become a Mason, which would be a valuable aspect of his nature for the remainder of his life, and the following decade he would continue to be a powerful speaker on subjects such as the railroad and Indian rights. With the Masons, he also helped found St. Johns' College. This was the first high learning institution in Arkansas.

As a friend asked for support for the idea of the South's secession from the United States, Pike plainly explained that "disunion would be such a remedy only as the death of the patient, which no doubt cures all his diseases."

During the mid-eighteenth century, many people left the East to head west and seek new lives. Perhaps it was for this reason that Newburyport in 1854 planned a "Homecoming" to take place on July 4, 1854. Invitations were sent out via newspapers, and prominent sons and daughters of the old town were contacted directly when possible. The idea was to see thousands of old friends who, although away, were just as much Newburyporters as ever.

Albert Pike, a very distinguished man by now, sadly declined the invitation:

> *I must very reluctantly forego the pleasure of once more visiting the old town, walking its well remembered streets, being greeted by the pleasant smiles of old familiar faces, and welcomed to my old home with the*

Albert Pike, seen here in his Masonic attire, was raised in Newburyport and considered it his old home, even after settling in Arkansas and eventually serving as a general in the Confederate army. *LOC.*

old hearty good humor and kindness…And I will not deny, but frankly admit that it would afford me the greatest pleasure, before I die, to address the people among whom I was born and reared, upon such an occasion as that of our National Anniversary. It would be the proudest day of my life.[19]

His estimated net worth in 1860, just before the war, was $40,000. He was then mostly calling himself an attorney, and his twenty-two-year-old son, Luther, was working with him. When the Civil War was just beginning, the Confederate government assigned Albert Pike to be commissioner of Indian affairs and to write treaties with the various tribes, as his skills seemed to dictate this post.

But in March 1862, General Albert Pike, CSA, led a portion of the left-wing attack of Confederates made up of Cherokee, Choctaw, Chickasaw, Creek and Seminole warriors against the Union army in the Battle of Pea Ridge. He would resign from the Confederate army in July 1862.

At least once did Albert Pike return to Newburyport for a visit. It was September 11, 1878, and he appeared at the second annual meeting of the Historical Society of Old Newbury. Luther Dame was chief marshal and historian, and that evening featured other speakers, but Pike made a brief address to the meeting. A large-framed man with long, flowing hair and beard was a commanding presence in any group he entered.

Pike's next major role would be in the realm of the Freemasons. Not content with the degrees, he recast them and raised the level of the position of the rites. His daughter said that he wrote little poetry his last twenty years but that it had been with him all his life. He died in Scottish Rite Temple, Washington, D.C., on April 2, 1891.

In 1901, the Masons erected a statue honoring Albert Pike in Washington, thus making him the only Confederate general with a statue in the nation's capital.

A lot of stories continue to this day regarding Albert Pike. He was liked and disliked. Some say that he, together with Grand Wizard and Confederate general Nathan Bedford Forrest, began the Ku Klux Klan. Although Pike was interested in secret rites and ceremony (such as the Klan had), hard proof of his involvement is difficult and sketchy at best.

One interesting story, though, with Pike was his claim to have shaken the hand of the Marquis de Lafayette when he passed through Newburyport in 1826 on his tour of New England for American's fiftieth anniversary.

CALEB HUSE: FROM THE COFFIN HOUSE TO THE CONFEDERACY

Another man from Newburyport became somewhat infamous for his actions in the Civil War—at least infamous for those of Northern persuasions.

Ralph C. Huse and his wife, Caroline Evens Huse, from Portsmouth, had a son on February 11, 1831. The boy, Caleb, was seven generations separated from one of the first settlers of Newbury, Abel Huse.

Young Caleb had an accomplished family in Newbury and Newburyport. His great-grandfather, Captain Samuel Huse, was famous for his time in the

Longtime property of the Coffin family, the Coffin House was used as a stop on the Underground Railroad. It was also the main childhood home of Caleb Huse, who ended up serving Jefferson Davis in the Confederacy. *NPLAC.*

Revolutionary War. Captain Huse was on the march to Albany that had led to Ticonderoga. Later in the war, he fought in the Battle of Long Island and at Dennis Heights.

When Caleb was four, Caroline died. The young boy was not motherless for long, though. Ralph remarried in 1837 in the Coffin House to Margaret E. Coffin. She died about a year later, and when Ralph was to be wed to his third wife, Sarah Stickney Barnard, Caleb went to live with the Coffins in the Coffin House.

Caleb was accepted to West Point at the age of sixteen and graduated in 1851, seventh in his class. His graduation included a rank of second lieutenant, and he was stationed in Key West, Florida. Here he served in the First Regiment, U.S. Artillery. Likely while here, he met his future wife, Harriet Pinckney, whose uncle was William Marvin, U.S. district judge at Key West. They were married in 1852, returning to her home state of New York, where the dashing young officer became the assistant professor of chemistry and mineralogy at West Point. He held this post from 1852 to 1859. This period at West Point included the time when Robert E. Lee was in command of the academy.

Caleb Huse took a leave of absence to go to Europe in 1859 but returned in 1860, taking the job offered as commandant of cadets at the University of Alabama. The school was introducing military functions and needed someone to organize and initiate the proper discipline. It wasn't easy, as the students disliked not only Caleb's strict nature but also the fact that he was from Massachusetts. Still, he was a credit to the university, and the men in power liked his results.

It was during a second leave of absence—not usually granted, by Secretary of War John B. Floyd (under President Buchannan)—that he was able to purchase guns, tents and other military gear for the university. This should come as no surprise, as Virginian John B. Floyd was already arming the Southern forts and arsenals while still operating under the title of U.S. secretary of war.

As Caleb had expressed his abolitionist beliefs as a cadet at West Point, we can only imagine the stunned reactions of family and friends when his signature appeared on a petition to reinstate the slave trade. The reactions must have continued once word reached Newburyport of the mission he had accepted from Jefferson Davis to go abroad and procure weapons and munitions for the newly formed Confederate government. Some sources say that he resigned in February, while others say March 1861. Either way, it was very close to still being a commissioned U.S. officer. His actions were likely the result of influence by his time at West Point under Robert E. Lee and other Southerners, as well as his time in Alabama.

With his experience as an artillery expert, Major Huse, CSA, went to Montgomery in early April 1861, just days before the attack on Fort Sumter. He then again sailed for Europe with hopes of procuring more matériel. After finding most of England picked clean by Yankee agents, he was later given complete power to buy whatever wherever he could.

Captain Bulloch, naval agent for the Confederates and uncle to Theodore Roosevelt, wrote after the war that Huse's actions in obtaining such items were of great importance in enabling the South to check McClellan's advance on Richmond in 1862.

After the war, Huse returned to the States in 1868 and attempted a variety of business ventures. Virtually penniless, he began a school in Upstate New York to prepare students to enter West Point. In 1879, the school moved to Highland Falls, New York. He died there in March 1905. Among his eight children at this time was a son who was an instructor at the U.S. Naval Academy at Annapolis.

During the war, Caleb's half brother, Ralph C. Huse Jr. of Newburyport, born to Caleb's second stepmother, Sarah, served the Union in the Third Regiment, New York Infantry, as a contract surgeon. He enlisted in September 1862 at the age of nineteen and served throughout the war. Brother Ralph was with the regiment during the Battle of Fort Fisher, North Carolina. In January 1865, a magazine exploded, and Ralph was seriously wounded.

Chapter 9

Homefront Newburyport

The residents of Newburyport followed the events of the war closely. Their sons had just left to answer President Lincoln's request for men to put down the rebellion.

Not long after the Cushing Guards first left for Boston and beyond, a collection was begun to raise money for the families of the men in service and also for the plan to begin a new company of soldiers.

George Lunt wrote a poem as the war began, and it appeared in the paper on Saturday, April 20:

"Our Country"

Our Country, right or wrong!
What manly heart can doubt
That thus should swell the patriot's song,
Thus ring the patriot's shout?
Be but the foe arrayed
And war's wild trumpet blown,
Cold was his heart who has not made
His Country's cause his own

Through fraction rule the halls
Where nobler thoughts have swayed,
One sacred voice forever calls

The patriot's heart and blade;
He, at his country's name,
  Feels every pulse beat high,
Wreathes round her glory all his fame,
  And loves for her to die!

Where'er her flag unrolled
  Wooes the saluting breeze,
Fling o'er the plain its starry fold,
  Or floats on stormy seas.
All the dearest things are there,
  All that makes life divine—
Home, faith, the brave, the true, the fair,
  Cling to the flaming sign!

Oh! Is this thought a dream?
  No! by the gallant dead
Who sleep by hill and plain, and stream,
  Or deep in ocean's bed;
By every sacred name,
  By every glorious song,
By all weak now and love of fame,
  Our country, right or wrong![20]

Charles Coffin answered the question made by women as to what they could do to help. He told them that if they knew how to sew, he wanted sixty-eight military coats and sixty-eight pairs of pants in one week. The women came forward, met at the Whitefield Church on State Street at the corner of Prospect Street and began sewing in the vestry.

Churches were decorated in patriotic colors, and sermons were full of loyal themes and often concluded with songs such as "The Star-Spangled Banner." Within days after the Eighth left, people were picking up the slack. The Newburyport Brass Band was in need of help, as five men had already enlisted by the third week of April.

On Thursday, April 24, the Brown High School hoisted an American flag under a special patriotic assembly. The Newburyport Brass Band played, and Caleb Cushing said words of encouragement later published in the paper.

The Newburyport National Guards were formed, then the City Greys and then the Seventeenth Massachusetts over the summer. During the war, the *Newburyport Daily Herald* employed a number of Newburyport's fighting men to be correspondents. These men wrote about their experiences and gave firsthand accounts of life in the army and battles. These men wrote under pseudonyms. One such man was "Essex." He first wrote to the paper in a letter written on April 19 and published on Monday, April 22, 1861:

> *Mr. Editor:—The 8th Regiment arrived in this city (New York) from Boston this morning at half past 6 o'clock, all in good condition, considering the fact that very little sleep could be had upon an express train. From the time of leaving Boston until we arrived in New York one continuous outburst of applause greeted the old 8th at every town and city. At Worcester and Springfield the enthusiasm was truly tremendous. All the buildings were illuminated in the vicinity of the depot; the military and firemen in a body were out, and salutes were fired from a park of artillery from the time we arrived until we left. Refreshments in abundance were showered upon us by the citizens generally. Gen. Butler, as true hearted a patriot as ever God breathed the breath of life into, who was called for at every stopping place; and cheers that rent the air when he appeared before the assembled thousands, showed that the people of New England are ready to appreciate the acts of her true hearted sons...*
>
> *It was reported that one man was killed by being run over by the train. This is not the fact. Every man who left Boston is still with us, and all are well and in good spirits. Company A, Captain Bartlett, now numbering 80 men, one of the largest companies in the Regiment; and if I mistake not, the feeling manifested by all his men, Newburyport will have no cause to be ashamed of her boys. We are off for Philadelphia, whence I will write again.*

Yours in haste, Essex[21]

"Essex" was George Creasey of the Eighth and Thirtieth Massachusetts and was one of thirty-one Newburyport soldiers writing the news back home. His son, George W. Creasey, would also serve in the war and prove his writing skill in a book at the turn of the century.

In the days before television, radio and Internet, the newspaper was the most important contact with the outside world. Newburyporters were in tune with the events throughout the country. They closely followed the events of

Baltimore and the fates of states such as Virginia as they seceded. News came from all over, including Sioux attacks out west as well as the death of Senator Stephen Douglas.

The pupils at the Purchase Street Grammar School took up a collection to go to helping the soldiers. Even the little ones wanted to help. In May, the city council began working out the amount, as well as a way to distribute funds for the relief of the families of the soldiers.

Also in May, Mr. D. Clark Batchelder sent a large box to the Cushing Guards in Relay, Maryland. It contained five regulation swords, havelocks for each soldier—sewn by the fine ladies of Newburyport—sheets, pillowcases and blankets for the sick or wounded, along with some items the soldiers desired to make life in the army more tolerable: tobacco, canned meats, stockings, handkerchiefs and other assorted articles. That all went after the package on May 4 of a box of items from the wives, children, parents and friends of the Cushing Guards. Cigars, tobacco, shirts, stockings and more went to Bartlett's men.

Albert W. Bartlett wrote a letter back thanking the kind people, but he mentioned that the Federal government had just distributed new uniforms for the men. These uniforms came with under drawers, shirts and stockings, and there was really no need for any more gifts as they were only serving ninety days. He wrote another letter on June 16, 1861, thanking the ladies again for the cakes, pillowcases, havelocks and blankets. Newburyport obviously wanted to help in any way.

By the summer of 1861, concerned citizens had mobilized. Mrs. Ruth Pettingell of 10 Bromfield Street (now 16–18 Bromfield) began the Soldiers' Aid Society. Ruth's son, Amos, would join the Thirty-fifth Massachusetts in 1862 along with Ruth's son-in-law, Thomas Cutter. On Tuesday nights, a group of ladies would meet at a given home, gather items and make packages of sorts for the soldiers. Bandages were wrapped for the wounded, and articles of food, socks or other necessary products that a soldier would need were packaged. This lasted for many months.

The Sabbath School and the Court Street Society held an exhibition on July 3, 1861, at the vestry full of patriotic music and tableaux. It was open to all. At about the same time, it was noted that through the Fourth of July, Mr. English's Company (actors) would be giving a performance of *Uncle Tom's Cabin*, featuring Miss Helen, who played the part of Eva.

With a war before them, it's not surprising that the *Newburyport Daily Herald* noted the less-than-enthusiastic mood of Newburyport that July 4. Roughly six thousand people gathered at the Bartlet Mall for patriotic music. Mr.

Wheeler of the Putnam School read the Declaration of Independence, and fireworks were lit near the Frog Pond.

It was a joyous occasion on August 1, 1861, as the first heroes, the Cushing Guards, came home. Still, others had left Newburyport, and for longer periods of time. By now, the idea of a short conflict between the North and South had settled into the reality of a much longer war with an unknown ending.

By the fall, the Eleventh Massachusetts had formed, also known as the McClellan Guards. The calendar year of 1861 saw many regiments formed; Newburyport men joined the Tenth, Eleventh, Twelfth, Sixteenth, Nineteenth, Twentieth, Twenty-second, Twenty-third, Twenty-sixth, Twenty-eighth, Thirtieth and Thirty-second Regiments. A company of sharpshooters, the First and Third Cavalry and the Fourth Battery of Light Artillery were added. Not counting the ninety-day men, Newburyport sent 450 men in 1861. That's just under 25 percent of the total who would eventually serve by war's end.

October saw what must have been a blow to many of the local families. The commonwealth deemed it appropriate to deny any funding to families whose sons or husbands served in other states' regiments. This included the Fortieth New York, aka the Mozart Regiment, which consisted of many Newburyport men. Following suit, the City of Newburyport also suspended funds.

A committee in mid-October met and wrote to suggest to the city council that if Massachusetts would not begin paying its sons for their efforts in the war, city hall should. Mayor George W. Jackman agreed and stated that $500 should be appropriated to the relief of families in the National Guards, Captain Westcott or any member of the Mozart Regiment residing in Newburyport.

In 1862, Jackman was mayor again. It was probably that February when the people of Newburyport first heard of General Grant. Fort Donelson had fallen, and even in the winter air, people gathered on State Street for the news. It was the first good bit of news that anyone could feel proud of regarding the events in the war.

Perhaps because of the positive news, a few days later the birthday of George Washington was celebrated with a bit more vigor. President Lincoln recommended that cities and towns plan events accordingly. Churches held services, flags were hung from windows and the house known as the Prince House posted a sign, "Our Guest of 1789," a reference to Washington's visit to Newburyport.

An early morning wake-up call got Newburyport excited. A telegram was received on May 26, 1862, at 1:00 a.m. by Albert W. Bartlett from the governor's office. All commanders and such were ordered to appear before the governor on Boston Common. By two o'clock in the morning, Bartlett, Adjutant George Creasey and Lieutenants Hodges and Collins were out rallying the men.

Alarms were sounded, and people were gathering on State Street to see the commotion. The Cushing Guards were ready at the armory by 3:00 a.m. and had left for Boston by the ten o'clock train. Two days later, it was determined by the governor that these men of Newburyport would not be needed at this time. Again the Cushing Guards, Company A of the Eighth Massachusetts, were ready when they were needed.

By the summer, Lincoln had called for more volunteers, and Governor Andrew stated that Massachusetts needed to contribute 15,000 of the 300,000 Lincoln wanted. Newburyport would have to present 179 men as its share. To help persuade new recruits, the idea of a bounty was initiated. At first it was to be seventy-five dollars, but then an additional twenty-five dollars was added to encourage men.

Fresh soldiers forming up in Brown Square, likely for inspection by Mayor Jackman before heading off to war. *HSON.*

By August, the money was doubled, and a bounty of $200 would be paid to every man who enlisted by August 11, 1862. The only stipulation was that they be between seventeen and fifty and pass the physical exam.

Bartlett was at city hall on August 6 as the recruits looking at the bounty were ready to sign their names for a three-year service. That day, Bartlett had 115 men on his roster. In the next few days, Newburyport had the quota. They were now the Thirty-fifth Massachusetts, Company B.

According to the postings in the *Newburyport Daily Herald*, the recruit who had a family also got a $114 relief for his family per annum. Even with a big incentive, patriotism

The young hero of Antietam, Albert W. Bartlett, was buried with full military honors at Oak Hill Cemetery. *WH.*

was still high—men were dancing in the streets, singing military songs and waving flags.

Joseph L. Johnson was put in command of the Cushing Guards, as Bartlett was now in another regiment. Another bounty was offered by the city for nine-month men for $100. It was then increased to $200. The Forty-eighth Massachusetts was recruited by Eben Stone.

After the bad news of Second Bull Run, the Soldier's Aid Society met on September 1, 1862, with nearly four hundred women at city hall for the purpose of preparing bandages for the wounded men. It was with deep sorrow that the news of the death of young Albert W. Bartlett reached Newburyport after the Battle of Antietam. He was not the first son of the city to die, but his reputation made his name far reaching.

Over the next few weeks, other men killed at Antietam were transported back to Newburyport and given military funerals. Fourteen men from Newburyport were killed or wounded between South Mountain and Antietam. In all, the battle was the bloodiest in American history, with roughly twenty-three thousand casualties in about twelve hours.

With a new year came a new mayor. Isaac Boardman was only mayor for one year before Jackman took over again.

Military funerals and news of the front continued to occupy the minds of many in Newburyport. In 1863, Governor Andrew was looking for proof that the men of Newburyport who had joined the Mozart Regiment of New York counted as part of the quotas required for the commonwealth. By the end of 1863, the quotas had been filled and the bounties had ended. Recruiting wasn't pursued as aggressively after that.

Jackman returned as mayor in 1864 and 1865. The city was reimbursed by the Federal government for the bounties issued because of a law enacted that allowed for government recruiters to gain bonuses for each man they signed. As Newburyport recruited its own, using its own agents, Governor Andrew used the money to help offset the expenses of the bounties. Some small bounties were used to entice men who might be drafted. Most men who would volunteer by now had already done so.

Life at home continued on with the headlines and soldiers' concerns until the spring of 1865.

Chapter 10

April 1865

Great News and Horrible News

It was almost over. Most people, at least those who followed the war, knew that things were winding down. All hoped and prayed that it would end with no more bloodshed. The concern, too, was the idea of guerrilla warfare, where the Rebels might live in the hills and among the populace and cause trouble, much like our modern image of the conflict in Northern Ireland.

On Sunday, April 9, 1865, the news arrived at about 10:00 p.m. to the people downtown near Market Square on the telegraph from the War Department:

Washington, April 9—10 o'clock P.M.

To Major General Dix

This department has received the official news of the surrender this day of Gen. Lee and his army to Lieut. General Grant, on the terms proposed by Gen. Grant. Details will be furnished as speedily as possible.

(signed)
Edwin M. Stanton, Sec'y of War[22]

Lee had surrendered to Grant! People couldn't contain themselves. Firecrackers were lit in the square, rockets were fired off, the City Cadets came out, bands played and someone fired a cannon. Thousands of people were in the area of State Street, near the *Herald* office and the telegraph. Buildings were illuminated. People began singing "The Star-Spangled Banner," "John Brown's Body" and other patriotic songs of the time. Cheers went up for Grant, Lincoln, Sherman and Sheridan. There had been enough blood. The crowd was out cheering until dawn.

Officially, the *Newburyport Daily Herald* wrote about it for Tuesday, April 11, 1865. The headline read "GLORIOUS NEWS! Lee and His Army SURRENDERED":

> *The surrender of Lee's Army is announced by the telegraph, and all will read for themselves. It is the most cheering news for years, the best that this generation has ever had, and in reality is the end of the war. All of the rebellion for months has been in Richmond in Jeff Davis and Lee. One week ago. Davis fled, and not having left his address, we have no means of knowing more about him. In all probability he will continue his flight to the other side of the Mississippi and out of the country. Now Lee—like a sensible man—has surrendered the confederate army of Virginia, and this must be followed by a general surrender. The end has come.*[23]

The euphoria the Newburyporters felt about the end of the war would be short-lived—they would feel completely different before the week was over. Although Lee's army had surrendered, there were still Confederates in the field, notably General Joseph E. Johnston, who was actually on the verge of surrendering to General William Tecumseh Sherman. Hope was high that this would take place soon.

Friday, April 14, was Good Friday. Most people in Newburyport honored Good Friday as they normally would. This coming Easter Sunday was one to be thankful for, but between the two days, news arrived that sent emotions into a tailspin.

It was no secret that President Lincoln enjoyed the theater. He and his wife attended plays during the war as a diversion from the sixteen-hour days he spent focusing on the war. Even by 1860s technology, photographs from 1861 until 1865 show a man who had dramatically aged.

On Friday, April 14, the Lincolns attended a play at Ford's Theater in Washington. The play, *Our American Cousin*, was a comedy, and as life was looking up, it seemed like a harmless bit of fun. The following morning, the telegraph office in Newburyport received the following news:

War Department, Washington

April 15, 1865, 8 A.M.

To Major Gen. Dix:

Abraham Lincoln died this morning at twenty-two minutes after seven o'clock.

E.M. Stanton, Secretary of War[24]

The news spread like wildfire. No president had been assassinated before, and there were many questions now. Would the war resume? Would bands of Rebels attempt other unheard-of actions? What was Andrew Johnson, the new president, going to do?

The *Newburyport Daily Herald* released an "extra" edition, the nineteenth-century version of "breaking news," and it was in everyone's hands. Lincoln was popular. In the November 1864 election, when Lincoln had run for a second term, Newburyport cast 1,076 votes for him and 522 for McClellan.

"Saturday morning brought us the sad intelligence of the most shocking crime in the annals of our history, and are not surpassed by any in the history of the world. It came like a shock from heaven upon the whole community, paralyzing the people that all business was suspended, and indeed with most persons, all orderly thought."[25]

The paper also mentioned that Johnson had been

The day the news arrived in Newburyport of Lincoln's assassination, the *Herald* rushed an extra edition to attempt to answer all of the questions the stunned residents had. *LOC.*

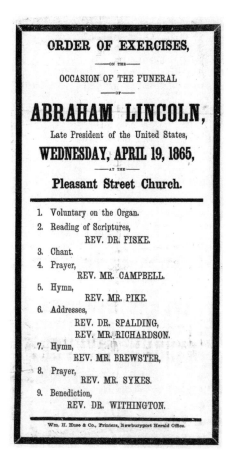

ORDER OF EXERCISES,
——ON THE——
OCCASION OF THE FUNERAL
——OF——
ABRAHAM LINCOLN,
Late President of the United States,
WEDNESDAY, APRIL 19, 1865,
——AT THE——
Pleasant Street Church.

1. Voluntary on the Organ.
2. Reading of Scriptures,
      REV. DR. FISKE.
3. Chant.
4. Prayer,
      REV. MR. CAMPBELL.
5. Hymn,
      REV. MR. PIKE.
6. Addresses,
      REV. DR. SPALDING,
      REV. MR. RICHARDSON.
7. Hymn,
      REV. MR. BREWSTER,
8. Prayer,
      REV. MR. SYKES.
9. Benediction,
      REV. DR. WITHINGTON.

Wm. H. Huse & Co., Printers, Newburyport Herald Office.

Wednesday, April 19, 1865, was a mournful day as Newburyport wept over the loss of Abraham Lincoln. Local churches held services. An overflowing crowd attended the Pleasant Street Church service, and each received an order of service like this one. *LOC.*

inaugurated and was now the seventeenth president of the United States. Some of the news had been rushed and incorrect, such as the arrest of Booth, who actually had created the largest manhunt in history up until that time.

Another dispatch announced that Lincoln's body was to be laid out in state at the White House. It was later divulged that Lincoln would be embalmed and that he and his son, Willie, who had died during his time in Washington, would both be taken back to Springfield, Illinois.

Details illuminated a most fearful evening, as not only was Booth after Lincoln, but another man had also forced his way into Secretary of State William H. Seward's home. Seward was in bed after a recent carriage accident. The intruder forced his way in and attempted to slice the secretary's throat. Seward had his daughter, a hired nurse and his son with him. His son was cut on the arm, and the nurse threw himself onto the attacker, who turned back and cut the nurse's throat. Mr. Seward was not killed and was able to easily identify the man.

Easter Sunday is a day usually spent in church on the topic of the crucifixion of Jesus and the resurrection. Instead, most churches in Newburyport tried to comfort their congregations and give some meaning to the recent events. At the Whitefield Church on State Street, the morning services on the topic of Lincoln's assassination were made by Reverend Spalding, Reverend Withington of Newbury and Professor Smythe of Andover Seminary.

On Monday, a meeting was held to decide what the city should do. Colonel Eben F. Stone was the chairman. A committee was formed, including Mayor George W. Jackman Jr., former mayor Isaac Boardman and others. A resolution was passed Monday night to acknowledge the events, to thank God that Lincoln had brought us through the war and to note that proper signs of respect would be expressed from city hall and the rest of Newburyport. Mayor Jackman recommended that all businesses be closed on Wednesday and that people attend their place of worship from noon to 2:00 p.m. All flags were to fly at half staff.

On Wednesday, April 19, Newburyport held its own funeral for Abraham Lincoln. By now, the city was dressed in black crepe from city hall to the engine house, as well as at private homes and businesses. Special services were held at the churches throughout the city, except for St. Paul's and the Universalist Churches, whose pastors were elsewhere. At noon, bells tolled. Guns were fired in a salute.

Mayor Jackman attended the special service held at the Pleasant Street Church (currently the Unitarian Universalist Church across from the post office) at 3:00 p.m. It became standing room only, and many could not get in for the crowd already in the church.

Afterward, the clergy of Newburyport wrote a letter to President Johnson. It was full of support for him and expressed to the new commander in chief the prayers from Newburyport and wishes for a return to more civil times.

Chapter 11

Yankee Homecoming

The war was over. Newburyport's surviving heroes came home and attempted a return to the lives they once knew. The city of Newburyport itself was proud of its veterans, and the city government decided to combine the nation's birthday with an extensive parade and reception for the boys in blue.

At sunrise on Tuesday, July 4, 1865, church bells began to toll, and a thirty-six-gun salute ensured that everyone knew what day it was. Compared to most local parades today, the reception parade for the heroes began early, at 9:00 a.m.

Planning had begun much sooner, and the streets were decorated in red, white and blue. At the head of State Street, an arch was erected with the mottos "Reunion To-day and Union Forever" and "The States—Distinct as Billows, but One Like the Sea." Down near Market Square at the bottom of State Street, another arch read, "Our Defense, the Breed of Our People, Stout and Warlike" and "Our Greatest Treasures—the Heroes of the War of '61."[26]

Five divisions formed up at High Street by the Bartlet Mall at 8:00 a.m. The chief marshal was Colonel Eben F. Stone. Before the first division, City Marshal Flanders ushered the event. Following him were various dignitaries, including Luther Dame from the City Cadets.

Among the four aides just before the First Division was Joseph E. Moody, the man who had endured a harsh life as a POW at Libby Prison and in Macon, Georgia, and up to Savannah. The First was primarily composed of civic organizations.

The Second Division was made up of representations from the various fire companies. Just as now, firemen in the parade were very popular with the crowd.

In the Third Division, featuring the army and navy, Captain George W. Creasey, son of one of the first volunteers and a soldier in his own right, was in the lead. One of his two aides was Thomas E. Cutter. After Creasey and the two aides, the Newburyport Brass Band, consisting of fifteen musicians, played patriotic and national themes.

The Fourth Division, though, got the most acclaim. This was made up of the soldiers and sailors who made Newburyport home. Some, who were disabled from the war, rode in carriages. Lewis A. Horton had lost both arms in the war, and he shared his ride with Daniel O'Grady, who had lost both of his eyes in service to his country.

O'Grady was an Irish immigrant to Newburyport, working as a weaver, who had enlisted in the Twenty-eighth Massachusetts, Company D (the Irish Brigade), and had been mustered in on December 13, 1861. He fought at Secessionville, South Carolina; Bull Run; and at Chantilly, Virginia. He also saw the South Mountain and Antietam battles in Maryland. He fought at Fredericksburg, where the Irish Brigade made the infamous charge up Marye's Heights. In the spring of 1863, O'Grady was captured at Chancellorsville. From here, he went to Libby Prison but was soon exchanged. He reenlisted in a veterans regiment and fought many more battles. A head wound at the Wilderness left him completely blind. Daniel would manage to find work and raise a family. He and his wife, Ann, would have four children, two boys and two girls, before he died on June 10, 1875. He was laid to rest at the Catholic cemetery off Storey Avenue.

By the spring of 1864, Lewis A. Horton was home in Newburyport after his discharge. He married his fiancée, Frances, and found sweet work as a confectioner. He and Frances had a daughter, Florence, within the first few years of marriage. Later, daughter Luella and a son, Aubin, would round out their family.

Horton's experience in the war was with the U.S. Navy on board the USS *Rhode Island*, which had varying duties during its time in the war. It served to chase blockade runners quite successfully, and it towed Monitor-class ships to the Carolinas. While towing the famous *Monitor* itself on December 30, 1862, a violent storm began, and the *Monitor* started to take on water, with the pumps not being able to keep up. Crewmen from the *Rhode Island*, including Lewis A. Horton, managed to save many of the officers and crew during the fierce storm. Eventually, the high seas and gale winds overtook the *Monitor* and, with it, four officers and twelve enlisted men. Newburyport man Lewis A. Horton was still on the open sea in the storm in a cutter from the USS *Rhode Island*. The high waves and strong winds continued, and it was many hours before help for Horton arrived. He was picked up by a schooner about fifty miles off the coast of Cape Hatteras.

At one point during his service, Horton had both arms blown off from a powder explosion. They were taken right off all the way to the shoulders. He was lucky to be alive. With his service and disability, the General Court of Massachusetts initiated on June 12, 1869, an annuity of $100 to Mr. Horton for the rest of his life. He also received a $25-per-month pension from the U.S. Congress, but it only lasted two years, with money coming from the naval pension fund. There was no Department of Veterans Affairs then. He joined the GAR and at one point served as commander. Horton died on June 8, 1916. He was buried in Jamaica Plain, Massachusetts.

The Fourth Division of the grand parade was a cross section of various trades in town, from the mills to factories and shipbuilding and such. It displayed the types of industry that a city like Newburyport produced. Newburyport was an industrial city and proud of it.

Finally, the Fifth Division had decorative pieces describing the struggle that the country had just gone through. Signs read "Liberty," "Thirty-Six States" and "Soldiers of 1776–1865," among others.

At 9:00 a.m., the parade began its trek through Newburyport. From the Bartlet Mall, the participants walked to State Street, heading to Market Square. At Market Square, they countermarched back up State Street to High Street, turned left onto High and continued to Bromfield Street. The length of Bromfield Street was marched to Water Street, near Joppa Flats. They turned left onto Water Street and walked over to Federal Street until they reached Middle Street, where they continued to Market Square again.

This time from Market Square, they went down to Merrimac Street beyond the downtown and over to Market Street. Up Market Street they worked their way back to High Street in the North End. Once on High Street, they continued until they got to Olive Street. They went down Olive Street past the Methodist church (now the synagogue) and one more block to Congress Street, and they then took Kent Street.

With a right turn onto Kent Street, soon they were back on Merrimac Street. A little farther down they went until they got to Broad Street, where they continued their parade up to the end at High Street.

Now they headed back toward downtown and turned onto Market Street just until Washington Street. This took them to their final intersection, where they came to Pleasant Street and the Pleasant Street Church (currently across from the today's post office), which held services.

Everyone then walked to city hall, where a large reception had been planned. Placed over the front door was a welcome banner. An evergreen arch just inside had written on it "Grant, Sherman and Farragut."

Nearly eight hundred veterans had dinner waiting for them to be served by one hundred female volunteers, who were only too glad to be of service. Mayor George W. Jackman Jr. said a few words, and then a prayer was said by Reverend Fiske. This was followed by descriptions of the men and their regiments from Newburyport and their service. Someone then read the Declaration of Independence, and another made a remembrance of Abraham Lincoln.

To continue the celebration into the evening, illuminations were lit, and at the Bartlet Mall, an estimated twenty thousand people came to watch the fireworks. A stack of arms and a drum on its side decorated the front of the mall, with another arch reading "Welcome Veterans." American flags adorned the arch as well. Many rockets took to the air that evening, to the crowd's delight; however, a number of other fireworks slated for the evening were accidentally shipped to Hull. As the paper wrote, as goes Hull, so goes Massachusetts.

Chapter 12

Postwar Years

GAR POST NO. 49

Almost every town in the United States had a GAR building or hall. Even the South eventually had them, as many former soldiers relocated to states that had been in the Rebellion.

What was the Grand Army of the Republic? To give it a more modern analogy, think of it as a combination of the Veterans of Foreign Wars, the American Legion and the Freemasons. It was a place where veterans would meet to discuss issues of their concern and plan ways to memorialize their fallen brothers.

In Newburyport, we are constantly reminded of these men when we pass by 57 State Street. There's still a sign on the front calling it the "Grand Army Building." But who were these men, and did they do anything in Newburyport worth mentioning? What was the GAR really?

To go further, we must consider the times. The war had ended; 600,000 American had died. The soldiers coming home to Newburyport and other towns were changed men. The scars weren't always visible on the outside. Horrific scenes of slaughter and suffering would haunt these men for the rest of their lives.

The United States government had no Department of Veterans Affairs to help soldiers cope or help wounded soldiers with medical needs (such as finding a prosthesis). No one, except for some local charities, was around to help with the widows and orphans too numerous to imagine who no longer

APPLICATION FOR CONTRIBUTING MEMBERSHIP.

To the Officers and Members of

A. W. Bartlett Post 49, G. A. R.,

DEPARTMENT OF MASSACHUSETTS.

The undersigned makes application to become a

CONTRIBUTING MEMBER OF A. W. BARTLETT POST 49, G. A. R.,

in accordance with the following resolutions:

RESOLVED : 1.—Any person may become a Contributing Member of this Post by the payment of an Annual Fee of Two Dollars: the first fee to accompany the Application, and payable thereafter January 1st of each year, the name of said Applicant having been presented at a regular meeting of the Post, and receiving a majority vote of the members present and voting at said meeting.

2.—Any person may become a Life Contributing Member by the payment of Twenty-five Dollars, ($25): the name of said person having been presented and accepted as provided in paragraph 1.

3.—A rejected Application shall be returned to the candidate, together with his fee for membership.

4.—All money received for membership fees and dues from Contributing Members shall be placed in the Post Fund.

5.—Contributing Members shall enjoy, with other members, the privileges of use of hall and ante-rooms when the same are not used for Post meetings, and may participate in all social gatherings of the Post on the payment of such fees as are paid by Regular Members; *provided* however, that no privilege herein accorded shall conflict with the Rules and Regulations of the Grand Army of the Republic or the By-Laws of this Post.

Name

Residence

Recommended by

Enclosed is Proposition Fee. $

To join the Albert W. Bartlett GAR Post No. 49, one had to fill out this application for review, as well as come up with the two-dollar annual membership dues. *WHC.*

had the breadwinner at home, especially during a time when women didn't often work outside the home.

The many needs derived from such a state led to the creation of the GAR. This organization sought to help out the families of soldiers and sailors who couldn't get by without some assistance. These groups also wanted future generations to remember the deeds of these soldiers.

From 1887, this receipt shows that the GAR hall was used much as modern VFW halls are used. The GAR member authorized to write the receipt was none other than Thomas E. Cutter of the Thirty-fifth Massachusetts, Company B. *WHC.*

In forming such a group, the veterans also found camaraderie and support. It was the GAR veterans who put up monuments across the country of Civil War soldiers or sailors. The GAR members also held reunions at battlefields to commemorate anniversaries of battles. Gettysburg and other notable battlefields are peppered with markers, monuments and statues, most of which were placed by members of the GAR.

The GAR claimed 400,000 members in 1890, with seven thousand posts. Presidents Grant, Hayes, Garfield, Harrison and McKinley were members. When President McKinley died in 1901, a committee was formed to participate in the funeral ceremonies. It was President Theodore Roosevelt who made sure that there was room for the five gentlemen to ride in McKinley's train. The GAR was also a great lobbying force.

The lasting influence the men of the GAR left us was to choose a day of the year to remember their fallen comrades. They called it Decoration Day and held it on May 30. We now call it Memorial Day and honor those from all wars who have fallen.

Above, left: GAR fairs, like this one at city hall, were held to raise money for the old gents to travel to reunions and cover expenses at home. *HSON.*

Above, right: On May 26, 1936, the *Newburyport Daily News* honored the last two members of the Albert W. Bartlett GAR Post No. 49. *NPLAC.*

In 1868, Captain J.T. Lurvey formed Newburyport's GAR Post No. 49, also called the Albert W. Bartlett Post in honor of the hero of Newburyport from the Eighth Massachusetts and later the Thirty-fifth Massachusetts who died at Burnside's Bridge at the Battle of Antietam in September 1862. Plenty of Newburyport men signed up for the post, and soon they had a permanent building. Salisbury didn't have a GAR post, so some of its veterans came to Newburyport's. Sadly, Edward F. Bartlett, the younger brother of Albert, never joined the post bearing his family's surname.

The building at 57 State Street was originally owned by Henry C. Plummer, who had a dry goods business for many years. Everyone called it the Plummer building back then. But on March 9, 1877, Post No. 49 purchased the building.

Bartlett Post No. 49 only needed the second and third floors of the building, leaving the first floor available for retail usage. By the early twentieth century, the first floor had become a ladies' millinery and undergarments retailer.

Whatever changes they made inside or out were dwarfed by the gale that hit the building in April 1882 and blew off the roof. At this time, the roof was redesigned and raised, and structural changes were made.

The offspring society of the GAR, the SUV (Sons of Union Veterans), took over the responsibility of the building as the numbers of the old veterans vanished. Financial hardships left SUV members no other recourse than to sell the building in 1966 to Arthur Page Insurance, which continues to own the building.

A Visit from Brave Ulysses

The Eastern Railway Station sat on Winter Street as the last building that northbound trains would see before crossing the Merrimack River on their way to Salisbury, into New Hampshire and Maine. A mood of extreme excitement was evident one fall day. A train heading to Portland, Maine, was to stop briefly, and a very important man was to speak to the crowd.

Ulysses Simpson Grant had earned a place in American history. The name of his boyhood home tells the story of his humble beginnings: Hardscrabble. A West Point graduate, Grant spent much of his prewar life trying to find his niche. After leaving the army, he tried one unsuccessful venture after another to support his wife, Julia, and his family.

After the war, Ulysses S. Grant took his popularity to the White House. Now he was serving the men of Newburyport who had served under him. *LOC.*

However, Grant had been a good soldier in the Mexican-American War, and his experience was what Ohio needed when he volunteered after the events at Fort Sumter. He said, "There are but two parties now: traitors and patriots. And I want hereafter to be ranked with the latter and I trust, the stronger party."[27]

Grant's victories in the war and rise to the rank of lieutenant general, a rank only previously given to George Washington, as well as his gracious actions at Lee's surrender at Appomattox, made him a very likely candidate for public office. In 1868, Grant was elected the eighteenth president of the United States.

On Tuesday, October 17, 1871, President Grant's train stopped at the Eastern Railway Station in Newburyport. While only here briefly, the moment was nonetheless exciting. Mayor Elbridge G. Kelly met the president, and as politicians can't be mute in front of an audience, he spoke a few words himself.

The men nodded, and Grant took a slight bow to the mayor as a local band began playing "Hail to the Chief." To honor the commander in chief, a local artillery company then fired a salute. Grant took little time from the public's course of the day, but the people who gathered were no doubt pleased. Many were veterans who just a few years before had been serving under this man to preserve the Union. Now, it was Grant who was serving those men.

The moment came and soon went. Grant's train resumed its journey to Portland, and the crowd dispersed. Grant wasn't the first or the last president to come to Newburyport, but he was one who meant a bit more to many on a level only they could understand.

MOZART REUNION

Reunions were a frequent occurrence. In 1876, the four Mozart, Fortieth New York, companies from Massachusetts descended on Newburyport for a reunion. Hosted by Captain James P.L. Westcott, the men were welcomed by Mayor Atkinson, the Cushing Guards, the City Cadets and others. The town was decorated as fellow Civil War veterans joined them. As they paraded through the streets, people cheered and waved. The men stayed at the Ocean House, at the corner of Titcomb and Merrimac Streets. The Ocean House was owned by Captain Westcott, and he most certainly footed the bill for the 60 men who attended the reunion. Out of the original 404 members, only 100 were living in 1876.

The night they arrived, there was a grand reception for them at city hall. The evening lasted for hours as a band played and many from the "first families" danced into the wee hours.

The steamer *Everett* was waiting for the veterans the next morning and took them upriver to the estate of Captain Westcott. Westcott had purchased Laurel Hill in 1863, and the estate was a perfect location for the banquet (Laurel Hill is now part of Maudslay State Park).

Next, the *Everett* took the men for a ride down the river to the mouth and to Plum Island, where the Merrimack meets the Atlantic. There they enjoyed a clambake and fish chowder at the Bay View House.

All good things must come to an end. The men finally headed for the train depot and said goodbye to Newburyport. But their first reunion was so good that they scheduled one a year later in Milford.

Other reunions took place in the decades to come. Some of the more extensive ones were held on special anniversaries, such as the 1913 reunion at Gettysburg, Pennsylvania. It marked the fiftieth anniversary of the battle, and about twenty-five thousand veterans attended from all corners of the country.

FEW REMEMBER

It was reported in the *Newburyport Daily News* on June 20, 1913, that Charles E. Hardy of 19 Olive Street (now 23 Olive) would be one of eight men attending this reunion. Hardy was born in October 1837 and served in the Twelfth Massachusetts, Company E. This regiment was in the I Corps of the Army of the Potomac.

The *Newburyport Daily News* of Tuesday, May 26, 1936, featured an article about the last two members of Post No. 49: Commander Charles F. Peel and Adjutant Charles T. Balch. It was days before Memorial Day, and the two men asked about the issued orders for the day. Peel was able to participate, but Mr. Balch was confined to his home with illness.

TRANSPLANTED VETERANS

America has always been a country on the move. As the years after the war rolled by, life in the United States moved on. People relocated to find new jobs, new lives and new starts.

Men from other towns and states would find themselves living in Newburyport in the latter part of the nineteenth century, and they would find their place in the city. A veteran of the Civil War who moved to town would likely check out the local GAR post to meet up with men who had similar experiences and perhaps form some good friendships. Many of these

The members of the Grand Army of the Republic, here heading up State Street and passing Essex Street in 1893, marched to honor their service and to remind people of the trials of war. *HSON.*

men set roots here in Newburyport, and it's very likely that many of their descendants still reside here.

Leroy G. Weston was one such individual. Leroy was born on April 17, 1842, in Chicopee, Massachusetts. When the war broke out, he was living with his parents, Rufus and Harriet Weston, in Tolland, Connecticut, where Leroy was a machine apprentice.

Leroy enlisted in April 1861 as a bugler for Southards Battery, Connecticut Light Artillery. It was for three months, and after ending in July, he reenlisted as a private in Company F of the Fifth Connecticut. He was in the Shenandoah Valley in 1862 under Pope, the campaign that ended with Second Bull Run. After being wounded at Cedar Mountain on August 9, 1862, he was discharged that December.

In 1863, he enlisted that July in Company C of the Third Massachusetts Artillery. But in August 1864, he was discharged for promotion to captain of U.S. Volunteers and was put in place to guard a railroad bridge on the Louisville and Nashville Railroad. He worked his way up to major by the fall of that year. He commanded a post at Murfreesboro and later Smithville, Kentucky, up until the end of the war.

Leroy Weston then joined the Liberal Army of Mexico in September 1865 as captain of artillery, and then as a major of cavalry in 1867, before resigning and coming back to the States in 1869. He moved to New Jersey, where he was a charter member of GAR Burnside Post No. 4 in February 1870.

Leroy then returned to a life in Tolland, Connecticut, where he worked as a woolen operator. Later, in 1877, the Westons moved to Providence, Rhode Island, and Leroy worked in a cotton mill. Before moving to Newburyport, he had three children from two wives. His wife, Myra, joined him in Newburyport.

On September 1, 1843, a baby boy was born in New Brunswick, Canada, named William C. Cuseck. William joined the American conflict on June 24, 1861, just three months before he was eighteen. He signed up from Methuen as a private in Company B, First Massachusetts Heavy Artillery. He served in fortifications around Washington, was detailed as an orderly and performed mail carrier duty as well. In the spring of 1864, he joined the Army of the Potomac under General Meade at North Anna River, Cold Harbor and Petersburg. William's term of service was up on July 8, 1864.

Newburyport offered William Cuseck a good place to raise a family. He and his wife, Mary, had a home on Low Street, where they raised their

Another occasion to march, with GAR Post No. 49 marching through Market Square in 1907. Note the young boy clinging to his grandfather's arm. *HSON.*

children, William Jr. and Nellie. William lived until November 23, 1932, dying at the age of eighty-nine.

Josiah E. Johnson, from Lowell, Massachusetts, served the Union as a private in the Fifth Ohio Cavalry. Over the course of his four years in the war, he was a bugler at various levels: company, regimental and battalion. He was with the Fifth Ohio at such battles as Shiloh, Tennessee, and Corinth, Mississippi, and in other skirmishes in that region. His term of service ended when he was discharged at Columbus, Ohio, on December 4, 1864.

By the 1880s, Josiah was working as a machinist in Newburyport, while he and his wife enjoyed the warmth of their six children at their home at 24 Lime Street. Josiah died on June 9, 1913.

A Maine man who enlisted from the state of Kentucky ended up residing in our Clipper City. Edward Sexton, born in Augusta, Maine, was twenty-one when the war broke out. He enlisted in Company F of the Fifth Kentucky Regiment. He participated in such battles as Shiloh and Tullahoma and at Chattanooga, Tennessee. In September 1863, he was involved in the Battle of Chickamauga, during which he was captured and taken as a prisoner of war.

Sexton spent time as a POW at Libby Prison and Scott Prison, both in Richmond. Later, while at Belle Isle, he was exchanged and able to return to his regiment. He was a participant in the action at Buzzard Roost Gap, Georgia, in early 1864 and then at Kennesaw Mountain, Lost River and Big Shanty in June. He was with General Sherman during the siege of Atlanta, but in September 1864, as he had completed his service, he left the army before Sherman's March to the Sea.

The typical soldier was in his late teens or early twenties. With the exception of officers such as generals, rarely were there men in their forties, but Stickney S. Gale was such an exception. Mr. Gale was a veteran of the Mexican-American War, having served on the frigate *Independence* sailing from Boston in August 1846 at the age of twenty-two. The ship engaged in battles at Acapulco, San Blas, San Marado and La Pasa. After his term, he was discharged in San Francisco, a long way from his birthplace of Sanford, Maine.

By the time the Civil War began, Stickney was married to his wife, Abby, and had two daughters, Maria and Sarah. The Gales lived a life in Chester, New Hampshire, when Stickney Gale, now a shoemaker, felt his patriotic blood churn. He enlisted in Manchester, New Hampshire, as a private but was mustered in as a corporal in Company K of the Fourth New Hampshire Volunteer Infantry on August 2, 1861, just three months before his thirty-

Turning onto High Street from State Street, these GAR vets passed the building (on left) that would one day hold meetings for doughboy veterans from World War I. *HSON.*

eighth birthday. This was a three-year enlistment. Gale's regiment would see combat in the Carolinas, Georgia and Florida, but at Drewry's Bluff, he was wounded and taken prisoner. He was sent to Libby Prison and later Andersonville in Georgia. He was exchanged on April 2, 1865, just as the war was winding down. He convalesced in Baltimore and then again back in Manchester.

For his service, devotion and patriotism, Stickney S. Gale received the Congressional Medal of Honor. He was discharged in August 1865. After the war, Stickney moved his family to Salisbury, Massachusetts, and he became a painter.

Dr. George W. Snow was born in Chelsea, Massachusetts, in October 1837. He was living in Hillsborough, New Hampshire, just before the war. But by September 1861, as he was needed, he was commissioned a surgeon for the Twenty-eighth Massachusetts Regiment, serving with the men in the Carolinas and in the Army of the Potomac. At Second Bull Run, he was taken prisoner in the hospital in addition to the men he was attending, but he was released along with the wounded men in about ten days.

Snow was at the Battles of South Mountain, Antietam and Fredericksburg, and soon after, in March 1863, he was promoted to the rank of major with the Thirty-fifth Massachusetts Regiment. Dr. Snow was with these men as they fought at the siege of Knoxville, Tennessee, and then at the sieges of

Vicksburg and Jackson, Mississippi. By 1864, he was brigade surgeon and was present at the Wilderness, Spotsylvania and Petersburg, Virginia, where he was in charge of Division Hospital. Dr. Snow moved to Newburyport and died on May 20, 1893, while being a proud member of GAR Post No. 49.

The last Civil War Newburyport veteran, who could place himself with General William Tecumseh Sherman and the famous March to the Sea, was James L. Bryant of the Thirty-third Massachusetts, Company C. For 120 days, Bryant and Sherman's army were constantly on the move. They participated in battles at Resaca, Georgia; Cassville; New Hope Church; and Kennesaw Mountain. By the end of the summer of 1864, they had captured Atlanta and soon began the famous march, arriving at Savannah in December.

In early 1865, they continued into the Carolinas, with Bryant being with the men the whole time. This young man from Jefferson, New Hampshire, had begun his experience much earlier. When the war broke out, twenty-year-old James L. Bryant joined the Twenty-eighth Massachusetts on October 24, 1861, out of Wareham as a musician in the regimental band. He was mustered out in 1862 and enlisted in the Thirty-third Massachusetts at Framingham, which was mustered into service at Readville on August 6, 1862.

As an older man, James L. Bryant participated in many of the veterans events in town. He was also good for telling the old stories of his time under General Sherman. *WHC.*

The Thirty-third was part of the Army of the Potomac, and Bryant was in combat at Fredericksburg, Chancellorsville and Beverly's Ford. But James L. Bryant also participated in the Battle of Gettysburg in July 1863. Soon after, he and the rest of the men were transferred to the Army of the Cumberland under Sherman. When it was all done, he proudly marched in the Grand Review in Washington, D.C., and was mustered out on June 11, 1865.

James moved to Newburyport in the 1870s with his wife, Annis. They lived and began their family at 27 Olive Street (now 31 Olive Street), one of a row of townhouses. James worked as an operative in a local mill, probably the one in the North End. The Bryants were not a stationary family, and perhaps as more children arrived, there was need to move and

After the war, James L. Bryant made his home in Newburyport. Mr. Bryant was a link to the famous "March to the Sea" by General Sherman while serving in the Thirty-third Massachusetts. When he passed away, Bryant was laid to rest at New Hill Cemetery. *EH.*

expand. By 1877, they were at 4 Eagle Street, and by 1880, they were living on Merrill Street.

Annis gave James three daughters and a son: Edna, Annis, Mary and Walter. By 1900, they were living at 8 Oakland Street, which was on the corner of Oakland and Walnut Streets, but it no longer exists. He was active in the Albert Bartlett GAR Post No. 49 and, at one point, was post commander. By the early twentieth century, with his family grown, James and Annis moved to Milk Street, and James took on the job as janitor of the GAR Post.

James died at his home at 1 Barton Street early in the morning of March 12, 1928, and Annis joined her husband in Highland or New Hill Cemetery just a few years after.

Many other men from places far away found a life here in Newburyport and were as proud of their community as those who enlisted on State Street or in Market Square. They did nothing but enrich the city. They gave us more cause to be forever grateful.

ATKINSON COMMON

Upon the death of Eunice Atkinson in 1873, the City of Newburyport was bequeathed a substantial parcel of land at the junction of Ferry Road, Mosely Avenue and Storey Avenue near High Street. It was to remain open space to be used by the people, forever known as Atkinson Common. Little if anything was done with the property for twenty years.

Finally, in 1893, the Belleville Improvement Society was formed, and extensive work was done to landscape Atkinson Common. The ground was graded, plants brought in, flowers planted and a fountain built. Benches were placed, and the grand park became a gem to Newburyport, as well as surely the envy of other towns.

In 1879, the first monument was erected on the battlefield of Gettysburg. It was for the Second Massachusetts Regiment, and soon the wave of plaques, tablets and statues would freckle the landscape of that hallowed ground.

At this time, the nation itself was feeling the need to remember the men and deeds of the great and tragic war. As the century was waning, the mortality of these heroes of 1861–65 was apparent. With this, almost every city and town began erecting statues and monuments to the men who served and the ones who didn't return.

Newburyport felt the same emotion, and in 1895, the idea of a statue was considered and commissioned. Artist Mrs. Theo Alice Ruggles-Kitson, wife of Henry Hudson Kitson, modeled, designed and made the statue known as *The Volunteer*. It was cast at the Henry Bonnard Bronze Company in New York.

Finally, on July 4, 1902, the statue was presented to the city of Newburyport and accepted by Mayor Moses Brown. The biggest contributor to the cause was William H. Swasey of Summer, Swasey &

As the new century began, Newburyport, like most communities, wanted to honor its sons who had helped defend the Union during the Civil War. The result was *The Volunteer*, by Mrs. Theo Alice Ruggles-Kitson, and it was placed in Atkinson Common. *NPLAC.*

Currier, whose business was located at 45 Water Street and Commercial Wharf. Also in the crowd were numerous members of the A.W. Bartlett GAR Post No. 49.

An identical statue was placed in the Vicksburg National Military Park (Mississippi) and dedicated on November 13, 1903. Aside from Mrs. Ruggles-Kitson, Governor Bates of Massachusetts, Commander Judd of the Massachusetts Department of the GAR and thousands of others were present. The Vicksburg statue was to represent the three Massachusetts regiments present at the Battle of Vicksburg: the Twenty-ninth, the Thirty-fifth and the Thirty-sixth.

It was a number of years before an addition was considered to accompany the figure of the soldier coming home from war at the Atkinson Common. June 17, 1913, was a warm and pleasant day, when the emotions ran high for this addition. A platform was constructed between *The Volunteer* and the new walls. The walls were cloaked in a red, white and blue covering that appeared flag-like.

As the band played "The Star-Spangled Banner," the crowd rose to its feet, and twelve children—grandchildren of some of the veterans present—

June 17, 1913, was a beautiful day, and the members of GAR Post No. 49, along with their families and dignitaries, were on hand for the dedication of the tablets listing the soldiers and sailors from Newburyport who served in the Civil War. *NPLAC.*

At the proper moment, grandchildren of the old gents unveiled the tablet names. The children were dressed as soldiers and sailors or, in the case of the girls, in bright white dresses with liberty crowns. *NPLAC.*

marched up to the wall. Each child stood near a tablet. The six girls wore white, with goddess of liberty crowns. The boys wore uniforms of Civil War soldiers and sailors. Their names were Marion Ayers, Elizabeth Hopkinson, Ruth Connelly, Katherine Pearson, Sadie Carter, Dorothy Greaton, Harold Page, Walter Hatch Strobel, Stacey Eaton, Norman Perry, John Cutter and William Plummer Lowell.

At the signal, each child pulled a red, white and blue ribbon and exposed the tablets. Music by the Windsor Quartet began with "Comrades in Arms." Soon that was followed by "Tramp! Tramp! Tramp!" and "Rally Round the Flag," which got many of the old gents to their feet to sing along.

The names of the 1,431 soldiers and sailors who had served their country adorn the bronze tablets. President Lincoln is remembered in his address at the Gettysburg Soldiers' Cemetery dedication. After speeches recalling key battles and places, the band played "America," the audience again rising to its feet.

As evening neared, activities moved to the GAR Hall on State Street. Food was offered and music was played, including soloist Miss Anita Noyes and the Grand Army Quartette from Haverhill.

A locally published verse in the years after the war conveys the sentiment that we should always remember what these men did:

From an early twentieth-century postcard, a familiar scene of kids climbing onto the cannons in front of *The Volunteer* could easily have been photographed today. *WHC.*

LEST WE FORGET—*the Spirit of '61*

When they fit for Gen'ral Grant ({shouted} by gosh)
When they fit for Gen'ral Grant
Those good old days
Beneath the Stars and Stripes
When they fit for Gen'ral Grant

also

For your happiness and prosperity
Which you may continue to enjoy[28]

Arthur Monroe Moody

Conclusion

Tom Brokaw in recent years called the World War II generation the "Greatest Generation." It's hard to argue when one thinks of the trials that this generation went through, from rising above the Great Depression and then reacting to the attack on Pearl Harbor through to the invasion of Normandy and eventually the dropping of "the bomb."

However, I think I'd argue that the Civil War generation, at least in its place in our history, has an edge over that one. These people saw the tearing apart of the country, both physically and psychologically. The war affected every corner of the country in one manner or another. Sons went to war and never returned. Husbands came home maimed and changed forever. A whole race of people was set free to begin the pursuit of happiness. This generation even had to deal with the shock of the first presidential assassination.

The most important outcome of the war was the preservation of the United States. For decades, regions and states threatened secession, either over a tax, a war or some other cause. Shelby Foote said long ago that the Civil War made us an "is" when we used to be an "are"—the United States *is* versus the United States *are*. The country was stronger and ready for the future.

Had the war gone the other way, proof would exist that any state could leave its alliance with its neighboring states—thus creating the good possibility of various European-style countries covering the North American map. Without the outcome of the Civil War, the twentieth century might not have had a United States to help the Allies in either of the two world wars.

The Volunteer, by Ruggles-Kitson, located at Newburyport's Atkinson Common today. *WH*.

Newburyport came through the crucible of the Civil War with plenty to be proud of. Many of its sons served their country proudly and with honor. Its shipyards played their roles in stemming the rebellion. Politicians and citizens encouraged and helped the soldiers and sailors and, when the war was over, remembered their sacrifices.

We had a female nurse, a new concept in these times, and two sons side with the Confederates. Mrs. Smith gave her life to the cause she believed in, and Pike and Huse, though you may disagree with their positions, fought for their beliefs as well.

The next time you watch a ceremony honoring veterans, don't forget that Civil War vets need remembering as well. It's not right that we might no longer honor them the way we always did just because the last veteran of the war is gone. They helped to bring us to where we are.

I thank you for your interest in history and local history.

Notes

Chapter 1

1. *Newburyport Daily News*, "Newburyport Honors One of Its Greatest Sons," July 5, 1893.
2. Ibid.
3. *New York Times*, "French's Statue of Garrison," July 4, 1893.

Chapter 2

4. Lampe, *Frederick Douglass: Freedom's Voice*, 65.

Chapter 4

5. Davis, Papers of Jefferson Davis, vol. 7.
6. Creasey, *Newburyport in the Civil War*, 35.

Chapter 5

7. *Newburyport Daily Herald*, "Notice from Gen. Butler," April 16, 1861.
8. Creasey, *Newburyport in the Civil War*, 16.
9. *Eighth Regiment of Massachusetts*, 74.
10. Schouler, *History of Massachusetts in the Civil War*, 77.

Chapter 6

11. Creasey, *Newburyport in the Civil War*, 216.
12. Ibid.

Chapter 7

13. Ibid.
14. Goodrich. *War to the Knife*, 8.
15. Moody, "Life in Rebel Prisons," *Newburyport Daily News*, April 8, 1897.
16. Ibid.
17. Ibid.
18. Ibid.

Chapter 8

19. Bragdon, *Report of the Proceeding*, 111.

Chapter 9

20. Lunt, "Our Country," *Newburyport Daily Herald*, April 20, 1861.
21. "Essex," "Mr. Editor," *Newburyport Daily Herald*, April 22, 1861.

Chapter 10

22. *Newburyport Daily News*, "Glorious News! Lee and His Army Surrendered," April 11, 1865.
23. Ibid.
24. *Newburyport Daily Herald*, "President Dead!" April 18, 1865.
25. Ibid.

Chapter 11

26. Creasey, *Newburyport in the Civil War*, 200.

Chapter 12

27. Grant, *Letters of Ulysses S. Grant*, 25.
28. Moody, "Lest We Forget."

Bibliography

A.W. Bartlett, Post No. 49. "Personal War Sketches." Newburyport, MA: 1890.

Allsopp, Fred W. *Albert Pike: A Biography*. N.p.: 1928. Google eBook. http://books.google.com/books?id=y7lpMrL1CZsC&pg=PA142&lpg=PA142&dq=albert+pike+newburyport&source=bl&ots=2vUpF8sp-c&sig=UCj0QE2l1lcDpHSkpWhjPbudyjI&hl=en&ei=hAyKSuXrLY2-4M9rv3L4P&sa=X&oi=book_result&ct=result&resnum=8#v=onepage&q=albert%20pike%20newburyport&f=false.

Biographical Directory of the United States Congress. "Cushing, Caleb, (1800–1879)." http://bioguide.congress.gov/scripts/biodisplay.pl?index=C001016.

Bragdon, Joseph H. *Report of the Proceeding, of the Occasion of the Reception of the Sons of Newburyport*. Newburyport, MA: Moses H. Sargent, 1854.

Central Arkansas Library System. "Albert Pike 1809–1891." http://www.encyclopediaofarkansas.net/encyclopedia/entry-detail.aspx?entryID=1737.

Cheney, Robert K. *Maritime History of the Merrimac Shipbuilding* Newburyport, MA: Newburyport Press Inc., 1964.

Civil War Naval Sesquicentennial. "Black History Month Highlight: Robert Blake." http://civilwarnavy150.blogspot.com/2011/02/black-history-month-highlight-robert.html.

Creasey, George W. *Newburyport in the Civil War.* Boston: Griffith-Stillings Press, 1903.

Currier, John J. *History of Newbury, Mass., 1635–1902.* Boston: Damrell and Upham, 1902.

———. *History of Newburyport, Massachusetts: 1764–1905.* Volume 1. N.p.: self-published, n.d. Google eBook. http://books.google.com/books?id=k8cMAAAAYAAJ&printsec=frontcover&dq=currier+newburyport&hl=en&ei=KCqbTu-LEoLh0QHozaDGBA&sa=X&oi=book_result&ct=result&resnum=1&sqi=2&ved=0CC0Q6AEwAA#v=onepage&q&f=false.

Davis, Jefferson. The Papers of Jefferson Davis. Volume 7. Transcribed from the original in the Library of Congress, Franklin Pierce Papers, Series 3. Washington, D.C.

Doyle, Jean Foley. *Life in Newburyport 1900–1950.* Portsmouth, NH: Peter E. Randall Publisher LLC, 2007.

Duncan, Robert Lipscomb. *Reluctant General: The Life and Times of Albert Pike.* New York: E.P. Dutton and Company, Inc., 1961.

The Eighth Regiment of Massachusetts at Chickamauga Park. Beverly, MA: Crowley and Lunt, 1898.

Essex [George Creasey]. "Mr. Editor." *Newburyport Daily Herald,* April 22, 1861.

GAR Post No. 49. *Souvenir G.A.R. Fair.* Newburyport, MA: self-published, 1915.

Goodrich, Thomas. *War to the Knife: Bleeding Kansas 1854–1861.* Mechanicsburg, PA: Stackpole Books, 1998.

Grant, Ulysses Simpson. *Letters of Ulysses S. Grant to His Father and Youngest Sister.* New York and London: G.P. Putnam's Sons, 1912.

Haskell, Caleb Niles. *The Newburyport Directories: 1849 through 1881*. Boston: Adams, Sampson and Company; and Newburyport, MA: Hosea T. Crofort.

Huse, Caleb. *The Supplies for the Confederate Army*. Boston: Press of T.R. Marvin and Son, 1904.

Irving, Ron. "Grievances: Feuds and Fancies in the Fair City of Newburyport." Newburyport, Massachusetts, compiled by author, 1995.

Lampe, George P. *Frederick Douglass: Freedom's Voice, 1818–1845*. East Lansing: Michigan State University Press, 1995. Google eBook. http://books.google.com/books?id=H9EcJhyBausC&pg=PA66&lpg=PA66&dq=frederick+douglass+newburyport&source=bl&ots=PTprvlKk50&sig=Ijs-36EF3qKh9iEqMAew89467Uo&hl=en&ei=AVWRSv-GWN9LBlAeLx7CfDA&sa=X&oi=book_result&ct=result&resnum=7#v=onepage&q&f=false.

Lee, Amos W. "'61–'65 Recollections of the Civil War." Unpublished, put into print for private circulation by Edward B. Lee and Christine G. Lee, 1913.

Library of Congress, Main Reading Room. "The Grand Army of the Republic and Kindred Societies." http:www.loc.gov/rr/main/gar/garintro.html.

Loring, George Bailey, and the Newburyport City Council. *A Memorial of Caleb Cushing*. Newburyport, MA: William H. Huse, 1879.

Lunt, George. "Our Country." *Newburyport Daily Herald*, April 20, 1861.

Massachusetts Historical Commission. *Historical Commission Survey*. Form B Building, form no. 360. Boston: self-published, 1980.

Massachusetts Soldiers, Sailors and Marines in the Civil War. Adj. General Vol. I–VIII & Index. Boston: printed at the adjutant general's office, 1931.

Moody, Arthur Monroe. "Lest We Forget." Accompaniment to group photo of Adams, Cross, Chute, Monroe and Moody, date unknown.

Moody, Joseph E. "Life in Rebel Prisons." *Newburyport Daily News*, April 8, 1897.

National Park Service, Department of the Interior. "35th Massachusetts Volunteer Infantry Monument." Antietam. http://www.nps.gov/anti/historyculture/mnt-ma-35-inf.htm.

Newburyport City Maps. Newburyport City Hall, Assessor's Office, Newburyport, Massachusetts, 2010.

Newburyport Daily Herald. "Bounty Notice." August 12, 1862.

———. "Bounty Notice." July 15, 1862.

———. "Celebration of the Eighty-Ninth Anniversary of the Declaration of Independence." July 4, 1865.

———. "The Cushing Guard." August 12, 1862.

———. "Death of a Heroine of the War." January 4, 1873.

———. "The Death of Capt. Albert W. Bartlett." September 23, 1862.

———. "Mozart Reunion." 1876.

———. "Notice from Gen. Butler." April 16, 1861.

———. "The President Dead!" April 18, 1865.

———. "Slavery." September 7, 1841.

———. "Volunteering." August 12, 1862.

———. " The Volunteers for the War." August 8, 1862.

Newburyport Daily News. "Death of George W. Creasey." July 4, 1905.

———. "General Albert Pike Dead." April 3, 1891.

———. "Gettysburg Convention." June 20, 1913.

————. "Glorious News! Lee and His Army Surrendered." April 11, 1865.

————. "Hon. George W. Jackman Dead." January 4, 1895.

————. "Newburyport Honors One of Its Greatest Sons." July 5, 1893.

————. "Newburyport's Part in the War." June 17, 1913.

————. "Tablets Unveiled; Many Veterans Welcomed Here." June 18, 1913.

New York State Military Museum. "40th Infantry Regiment: Civil War." http://dmna.state.ny.us/historic/reghist/civil/infantry/40thInf/40thInfMain.htm.

New York Times. "Col. Caleb Huse Dead." March 13, 1905.

————. "French's Statue of Garrison." July 4, 1893.

————. "Monument at Vicksburg." November 15, 1903.

————. "Personal." April 2, 1864.

————. "President Roosevelt Honors the G.A.R." September 17, 1901.

————. "A Rebel Diplomatist-Sketch of Caleb Huse." April 10, 1864.

Noyes, Henry E., Colonel, and Harriette E. Noyes. *Descendents of Nicholas Noyes.* Boston: members of the New England Historic Genealogical Society, 1904.

Ohio Family Roots. *1890 Union Veterans Special Census, Essex County, Massachusetts.* Compiled CD-ROM, 2011. In author's collection.

P. Preservationist. "House Stories—79 Federal—Richard Plumer House," April 7, 2010. http://ppreservationist.wordpress.com/2010/04/07/house-stories-%E2%80%93-79-federal-%E2%80%93-richard-plumer-house.

Sargent, A. Dean. *Grand Army of the Republic, Civil War Veterans, Dept. of Massachusetts 1866–1947.* Compiled CD-ROM. Bowie, MD: Heritage Books, Inc., 2002.

Schouler, William. *A History of Massachusetts in the Civil War.* Boston: E.P. Dutton and Company, 1868.

Soldier's and Sailor's Memorial Hall Association. *Souvenir.* Newburyport, MA: self-published, 1917.

Swift, Lindsay. *William Lloyd Garrison.* Philadelphia: George W. Jacobs and Company, 1911.

U.S. Census Records. Essex County, Massachusetts, 1840 through 1930. Heritage Quest On-Line.

———. Pulaski County, Arkansas, 1860. Heritage Quest On-Line.

U.S. Department of the Interior. "Poet, Shoemakers, and Freedom Seekers." Salem Maritime National Historic Site, 2010. http://www.nps.gov/sama/historyculture/upload/UGRRsm.pdf.

U.S. Department of the Navy, Naval Historical Center. "USS Kearsarge vs. CSS Alabama 19 June 1864." http://www.history.navy.mil/photos/events/civilwar/cw-cru/kear-ala.htm.

U.S. Department of the Navy, Naval Historical Center. "USS Marblehead (1862–1865)." http://www.history.navy.mil/photos/sh-usn/usnsh-m/marblehd.htm.

U.S. Department of the Navy, Naval Historical Center. "USS Rhode Island (1861–1865)." http://www.history.navy.mil/photos/sh-usn/usnsh-r/rhode-i.htm.

Veterans' Grave Registration Records. City of Newburyport, WPA Project # 20169.

Index

A

Adams, Captain John
  G.B. 67
Andrew, Governor John
  A. 28
Annapolis 34, 53, 56, 77
Antietam 36, 46, 48, 54,
  85, 93, 99, 106
Appomattox 57, 100
Army of the Potomac 36,
  52, 54, 65, 102,
  104, 106, 107
Atkinson Common 109,
  110

B

Baltimore 11, 12, 13, 18,
  26, 33, 34, 48, 53,
  56, 82, 106
Baltimore and Ohio
  Railroad 34
Barker, Lieutenant
  George 32, 34
Barlow, Joseph 32, 53
Bartlet Mall 82, 92, 94, 95
Bartlett, Albert W. 30,
  31, 32, 34, 36, 38,
  46, 48, 54, 55, 56,
  82, 84, 85, 99

Bartlett, Horace W. 32
Baxter, Samuel 32
Belleville Improvement
  Society 109
Black, John 51, 52
Blake, Robert 43
Boardman, Isaac 39,
  85, 91
Boston 12, 13, 14, 18,
  26, 32, 33, 43, 44,
  56, 61, 65, 71, 72,
  79, 81, 84, 105
bounty 84, 85
Brooklyn 57
Brown, Captain
  Lawrence W. 40
Brown, John 13, 59, 88
Brown Square 13, 15
Brown's Wharf 42
Bryant, James L. 107
Burnside, General
  Ambrose 36
Burnside's Bridge
  (Rohrbach Bridge)
  48, 99
Butler, Benjmain F. 28

C

Chancellorsville 57, 93,
  107

Charleston 15, 26, 31,
  42, 54, 68
Chute, Richard 67
City Cadets 60, 92, 101
city hall 14, 39, 83, 85,
  91, 95, 101
Coffin House 24, 75, 76
Cold Harbor 53, 57, 65,
  104
Collins, John A. 18, 21
Collins, Nathan W. 32
Confederate States of
  America 28
Creasey, George 32, 54,
  81, 84
Creasey, George W. 54,
  55, 67, 81, 93
Cross, Henry M. 67
CSS *Alabama* 40
Cuseck, William C. 104
Cushing, Caleb 11, 16,
  25, 26, 29, 57, 80
Cushing Guards 26, 30,
  31, 32, 34, 38, 53,
  57, 62, 79, 82, 83,
  84, 85, 101
Cutter, Thomas E. 46,
  93

D

Dame, Luther 52, 58, 59, 60, 61, 63, 75, 92

Davenport, Moses 30, 39

Davis, Jefferson 26, 28, 77

Dodge, Richard S. 32

Dodge, William H. 32

Douglass, Frederick 13, 18, 19

Douglas, Stephen A. 26

E

Eastern Railroad 21

Eighth Massachusetts 32, 53, 56, 62, 84, 99

Eleventh Massachusetts 52, 60, 63, 83

Everett, Edward 26

F

Faneuil Hall 13, 14, 26, 32

Farley, William 42

Fifty-ninth Massachusetts 65

Flander, Nehemiah 31, 57

Fortieth New York 57, 83, 101

Fort Lee 62

Fort Pickering 62

Fort Sumter 31, 51, 77

Forty-eighth Massachusetts 65, 85

Fredericksburg 54, 57, 93, 106, 107

French, David M. 16

Frost, John S. 32

Fugitive Slave Act 22

G

Gale, Stickney 105

GAR Post No. 49 63, 96, 99, 108, 110

Garrison, William Lloyd 11

Georgia 42, 51, 54, 67, 69, 92, 105, 106

Gettysburg 50, 51, 57, 98, 102, 107, 109, 111

Giles, Nathan R. 32

Goodwin, Stephen H. 32

Grand Army of the Republic (GAR) 47, 55, 61, 65, 96

Grant, Sanford. W. 32

Grant, U.S. 15, 29, 32, 54, 83, 87, 88, 95, 98, 100, 101, 112

H

Harpers Ferry 13, 56

Harvard 25, 71, 72

Hastings, Captain 67

Historical Society of Old Newbury 75

Hodges, Lieutenant G. 32

Horton, Lewis A. 93, 94

Huse, Caleb 75, 77

Huse, Ralph C. 75

Huse, William H. 16

I

Indianapolis 56, 62

J

Jackman, George W., Jr. 39, 42, 91, 95

Johnson, Joseph L. 32, 55, 56, 85

Johnson, Josiah E. 105

Johnson, President Andrew 55

K

Kansas 13, 58, 59

Kossuth 50, 51

L

Lang, Thomas E. 32

Lee, Amos W. 48, 50, 51

Lee, Robert E. 15, 76, 77

Libby Prison 54

Liberator 13, 15

Lincoln, Abraham 26, 28, 29, 30, 31, 34, 51, 52, 55, 69, 79, 83, 84, 88, 89, 90, 91, 95, 111

M

Market Square 34, 87, 92, 94, 108

Marshall, Thomas E. 32

Masons 73, 75

McClellan, General George B. 36

Medal of Honor 42, 106

Memorial Day 98, 102

Mexican-American War 26, 28, 73, 100, 105

Miller, James 43

Moody, Joseph E. 65, 69, 70, 92

Morrison, Charles P. 32

Mozart Regiment 56, 57, 83, 86

N

Newburyport Brass Band 80, 93

Newburyport Daily News 102

Newburyport Fire
Department 52
Newburyport Herald 11
New England Anti-
Slavery Society
13, 14
New Hill Cemetery 52,
108
New York City 33, 44,
50
New York Draft Riots 50
New York Times 16, 17
North Carolina 44, 53,
54, 56, 62, 69, 78
Noyes, Ebenezer 61, 62
Noyes, George S. 62
Noyes, Joseph H.W. 61
Noyes, Josephine H. 61

O

Oak Hill Cemetery 38,
47, 56, 61, 62, 70
O'Grady, Daniel 93

P

Perley, John A. 32
Petersburg 53, 57, 104,
107
Pettingell, Amos 46, 47
Pettingell, Ruth 82
Pierce, Franklin 26
Pike, Albert 71, 72, 73,
74, 75
Pleasant Street Church
38
Plumer, Richard 21, 22,
24
Portsmouth 16, 21, 42,
50, 75
Pratt Street Riot 33

R

Ruggles-Kitson, Mrs.
Theo Alice 109

S

Salem Harbor 38, 60, 62
Semmes, Captain
Raphael 40
Sexton, Edward 105
Shaw, Joseph L. 32
Sherman, General
William T. 67, 68,
69, 88, 95, 105,
107
Sixtieth Massachusetts
38, 62
Smith, Sarah E. 63, 64
Snow, Dr. George W.
106
Sonora 40, 41
South Carolina 26, 42,
51, 54, 59, 68,
69, 93
South Mountain 36, 46,
47, 54, 85, 93,
106
Spotsylvania 54, 65, 107
Stone, Eben F. 56, 90, 92
Stono River 42
Swasey, William H. 15,
109

T

Temple Street Church
18
"The Star-Spangled
Banner" 80, 88,
110
The Volunteer 109, 110
Thirty-fifth Massachusetts
34, 46, 48, 54, 82,
99, 106
Todd, Francis 12, 13, 14
"To My Birthplace"
(sonnet) 17
Twenty-eighth
Massachusetts 93,
106, 107

U

Underground Railroad
18, 22, 24
U.S. Naval Academy 34,
43, 77
USS *Ascutney* 44
USS *Constitution* 34
USS *Kearsarge* 42
USS *Marblehead* 42, 44
USS *Rhode Island* 93, 94

V

Van Moll, Richard 32
Vicksburg 52, 54, 107,
110

W

Washington 26, 29, 34,
45, 46, 53, 55, 56,
64, 75, 87, 88, 89,
90, 104, 107
Westcott, James P.L. 56,
57, 101
Weston, Leroy G. 103
Whitefield Church 80,
90
Whittier, John Greenleaf
12, 15, 16, 24
Wilderness, the 54, 57,
65, 93, 107

About the Author

A former radio announcer turned writer, William Hallett is a twelfth-generation descendant of a first settler of Newbury, Nicholas Noyes. Always a fan of American history, Bill lived in Maryland near Pennsylvania as a youth and by his twenties had acquired an interest in Civil War history, which is so prevalent in that region.

In 1994, he returned to New England and not long after became involved in the Civil War Roundtable of New Hampshire. He led that group as president for ten years and as vice-president for two. He also joined the Civil War Roundtable of the Merrimack and served on the board. During the same time, he was introduced to the world of reenacting, with his first occasion being an encampment on the grounds of Gettysburg National Military Park in June 1994.

Determined to keep alive the memory of the people and events of this most crucial time in history, Bill has decided to create this book hoping to spotlight Newburyport's place in Civil War history.

Bill lives in Newburyport with his wife, Elizabeth. The couple periodically hosts Footsteps of Heroes: Civil War Walking Tour of Newburyport.